MONTANA
HOMESTEAD

---❖---

How I Built My Homestead Off Grid In The Wilderness

Gordon Blaine

SARCO PRESS

Copyright © 2015 Sarco Press

ISBN-13: 978-1506155951

ISBN-10: 1506155952

For Dad, who I realized too late
was the most generous person I had ever known;
and for Mom, who taught me to always
look at the bright side of things
and to laugh about the hard times.

CONTENTS

INTRODUCTION

I N THE BEGINNING I had no plans to write a book like this. I am a relatively private person and while I do keep up with the news and world events I do that from a distance. I prefer to spend my own time with my family and my dogs, walking my woods or operating my sawmill or reading my books in the cabin.

Years ago, my worldview shifted. I realized that the governing bodies were chipping away at our personal freedoms and I thought about how fragile our national economic system had become. Our way of life seemed balanced on the edge of a razor and it could totter at any moment. These weren't things that I thought about constantly but they were always in the back of my mind. I didn't discuss my thoughts with anyone except my wife, and she understood.

I began to prepare. I stored food and saved ammunition. I started a garden and taught myself how to process canned food. I saved things I thought we might need like vitamins , aspirin, soap, matches and lantern oil.

I didn't want to depend on our country's fragile infrastructure. But it always seemed as if there was something more I could do, as if I was missing some invisible vital step.

I found myself daydreaming of homesteading in the wilderness on a remote mountain somewhere.

When I was young my parents always had a garden but they were not what you would think of as homesteaders or farmers.

However, both my parents were raised by the Amish and had a lot of farming and primitive living experience.

Nowadays I feel like I am returning to my roots. As a child I spent many weeks with my Amish grandparents and cousins. One of my earliest memories is of drawing water from a hand pump, or staying at homes with no indoor plumbing or electricity, or of watching my grandfather plow a field with a horse-drawn plow.

I was a kid at these times and having had exposure to this all my life, I didn't see anything extraordinary about it. In fact I had a lot of fun, playing with my cousins in the hay barn or in the woods or riding to town in a horse drawn buggy.

Then in my adventurous years as a young adult I wanted to live in the big city by the ocean. As I got older and had children, I was drawn back to the lifestyle of my family before me. I thought about how nice it would be to return to a life like I had experienced in my youth.

In 2011 my wife and I both had decent jobs. We also had a big mortgage payment and car payments. We spent money on movies, restaurants, nice cars and the latest electronic gadgets. We were living the good life, in our dream state of Montana.

Then everything changed.

PART ONE
THE BEGINNING

East Coast

I<small>N</small> M<small>ARCH OF</small> 1995 I was working for a military communications contractor in the state of New Jersey. I was former military and carried a Secret security clearance. For the previous five years I had been traveling to different military bases to install LAN/WAN infrastructures, and in March I was working in New Jersey at Naval Air Engineering Station Lakehurst - the site of the famous Hindenburg crash. It was while working on this job that I met my wife. As a member of a British family, she had immigrated to the US at the age of 11.

We later married and had three kids. By 2002, we had started a family and settled down. We bought a house in the center of a huge subdivision on the busy east coast, with neighboring houses only a few feet away from our own.

Crime in our part of town had seemed to be getting worse. We had been hearing about some homes being broken into in distant parts of the subdivision. This caused in me a feeling of hopelessness, and I imagined thugs breaking my door down, and I would be helpless to protect my wife and young children. I brought up the idea of getting a gun for home defense and the idea was nixed. My wife felt that with small children in the house the idea was too dangerous. She was from England, and was not familiar with guns and she was somewhat afraid of them. I myself hadn't shot a gun in what seemed like decades and I had never owned one.

Meanwhile our worldview was shifting. It wasn't a sudden switch or potential disaster that triggered the change in our thoughts - it was more of a gradual broadening of our horizons. I began to see and think about things that I never thought about when I was a fun-loving, carefree bachelor. We paid attention to the news, to crime and politics and the gradual removal of our personal liberties. We were starting to think about the bigger picture.

It seems that when some of us become parents, we start to think about how we can take care of our kids no matter what happens. When I thought about that and followed it to its logical conclusion, I realized we can't protect them from everything, but we still should do everything we can.

A series of events occurred where I had traded a puppy for a Smith & Wesson .357, and this led to my bringing a gun home without telling my wife. I didn't hide it from her. I convinced her that I would keep it locked up and out of reach. I showed her how the safety locking mechanism worked and eventually she relented and didn't force me to sell the gun.

Later we went to the gun range and I taught her how to shoot. We brought along our oldest son, who was nine years old, and he put a few rounds down range as well. All three of us had a good time.

The act of practicing with the gun and handling it lessened my wife's fear of it. I think she began to understand that a gun is a thing which in the wrong hands can be dangerous, but with knowledge and common sense can be a safe form of self-defense. We felt better having a gun in the house.

Owning that first gun had a positive effect on us. We felt empowered, as if we really could do something to make our lives more safe. I began to wonder what else we could do to make our lives safer.

I have always been a voracious reader and around that time I read The Big Sky, by A.B. Guthrie. I became lost in the mountains, the wildlife and the sense of freedom and adventure. So on our next vacation we drove 2,600 miles to Montana and spent time at Glacier National Park, and Yellowstone National Park. We fell in love with the beauty of the area and we thought it would be a better place to raise the kids. We decided that when my wife finished nursing school we would pack up the kids, the dogs and all our belongings and move.

And in June of 2006 we did it.

Montana

IN SEPTEMBER OF 2006 we bought a house with 4 acres located within the city limits of a small Montana town of 800 people. It was a nice place with a creek and a small grassy pasture. My wife's parents came out to visit from Florida and fell in love with the area. To our delight, they decided to move to the neighborhood and shortly thereafter they did.

We loved our new home, but a fear nagged the back of my mind. The house payments, car payments, and other expenses were enough that it took both our incomes to pay the monthly bills and we didn't have money left over to save. My wife had a good job and I had a halfway decent job so we were keeping afloat, but just barely. We had a good life but like so many other people we were living paycheck to paycheck.

That is when I began to store food. I would buy canned food by the case; vegetables, fruit, tuna and spaghetti sauce. I built a nice wooden can rack, where I could put new cans in the top and pull out the older cans from the bottom. It held hundreds of cans, and I kept it full.

As I researched ways to store food I learned about saving bulk quantities of food in five gallon buckets. Over time I bought dozens of buckets and lined them with food grade mylar bags and filled them with wheat, rice, beans and macaroni noodles. I sealed them up with an oxygen absorber and took them to my wife's parents' house where I stored them in a root cellar.

I also added to my small collection of guns and taught myself how to reload ammunition. Eventually I started casting my own lead bullets and I built up a small stockpile of lead.

Meanwhile I worked on my garden. I had the best luck with raspberries and strawberries but I also grew tomatoes, a little corn, and a few other things. I didn't get much out of those vegetables but I was learning.

We started raising some chickens, and we had good luck with them. Later we got a couple of kid goats, thinking someday we would begin milking them.

I kept the lawn mowed, installed sprinklers and fenced in the whole acreage and generally worked on improving the property.

I felt as if we were living the good life. The kids had friends over for birthday parties and our relatives came to visit from out of state. If I ignored the nagging feeling in the back of my mind I felt pretty good.

In 2011 a series of mundane events caused us to lose it all. I lost my job and got another, lower paying job. The same happened to my wife. Suddenly we realized we could no longer make the house payments or the car payments. We tried to work something out with the banks but they were not interested. Before we knew it we had lost the house and the car and were living in our old camper in the backyard of my in-laws.

It was truly an eye opening experience. The worst had happened and we had survived. But it was only because of the generosity of my wife's parents that we had a place to live. What if they had not been there to support us?

THE SHIFT

I N THE YEAR OF 2012, my wife and I were stuck in a difficult situation. Neither one of us had a decent job and we were living in her parent's back yard in an old camper. The oldest of our three kids was off in the military but we still had to take care of our fourteen year old daughter and our fifteen year old son. The kids were able to live inside the house with the in-laws but there was not enough room for my wife and I and the dogs. So the two of us lived in the camper, even through the harsh Montana winter where the temperature plummeted to below zero.

But it wasn't so bad.

During those times I did a lot of reading. We gained an awareness of Monsanto GMO food and beef feed lots and herbicides and pesticides and chemical fertilizers and the destruction of the earth's topsoil by industrial scale monocrop farming. We figured none of these things were good. I had plenty of time to read and I discovered the concepts of organic gardening and permaculture and no-till gardening.

We fantasized about owning our own land, where we could do whatever we wanted and the bank couldn't ever take it away from us. We could grow huge gardens of organic food, raise chickens and beef cows, and build our own house. We decided to do what we could to gain an independence of the things we didn't like, and to become as self sufficient as we can so that we would not have to rely on the fragile infrastructure that tenuously held everything together. We had no cash to accomplish any of those goals. But we had the dream.

I did have a small 401k retirement account into which I had put money for the last twenty years. It wasn't really enough to retire on but there was about ninety thousand dollars in it and that gave us a small feeling of security. Of course our biggest worry was what would happen in the next few months. Retirement seemed like a distant worry.

It seemed like we had two options. The first option was to find new jobs and get back on our feet, but at a much lower quality of life than what we had been used to, and with rent or mortgage and utility bills and everything else; in other words, get back into the rat race. I was in my forties - if by some miracle I would be able to gain a new mortgage I felt I would die of old age before it was paid off. So that idea didn't appeal to me.

The other option was a little more far-fetched.

We would find a piece of land, drill a well and build a house. We would cash in the 401k account to pay for it all. After all, what good was a retirement income if it only paid the mortgage or the rent and we still had to pay for groceries and utility bills?

Then we might have the chance to grow gardens and raise livestock to provide food. I imagined sprawling food forests and huge pastures for pigs and beef cows, and beehives and a kitchen herb garden and wild rose hips growing outside the door.

Once before, we had picked up everything we had and moved cross-country. Most people would balk at this idea, finding a hundred reasons why they can't do it. But we had done it once so we knew that we could do anything we wanted if we set our minds to it.

So we followed through with our dream.

PART TWO
THE FIRST YEAR

Fall 2012
The Land

W<small>E SEARCHED FOR LAND</small> for months in the papers and on the internet real estate web sites. We walked dozens of properties. We soon learned that the properties within our budget were going to be either very small or come with restrictions on what we could do. None of the properties we looked at seemed to have everything we were looking for.

Our potential property had to meet certain criteria. I printed a list of those and gave it to our local real estate agent.

- Southern exposure for gardening
- If no grid utilities, must have cell phone reception
- Year round access, given that a four wheel drive vehicle may be required
- Good potential for a well and septic system
- No restrictions or covenants
- Limited building codes
- Full water, mineral and timber rights
- At least 5 acres
- Some flat terrain for building and gardening.
- Seclusion

I felt that if we could find a piece of land that met all those requirements we would have good potential to develop it into our dream property. It took us a long time to find that land. Our real estate agent was finding nothing and my wife and I were doing most of the leg work, making calls and setting up appointments. But in the end, in September of 2012, it was our agent (Dave) who found the property. Once we paid a visit to the site we knew we had found what we wanted.

It was 20 flat acres located a little bit east of Idaho and within 10 miles of a major interstate (although most of those miles were on back country dirt roads that see little traffic). There were no springs, ponds or creeks on the property but there was a major river within a mile (as the crow flies) and a year-round creek closer than that. In addition, a well had already been drilled and cased, which eased my worries quite a bit. I knew that it can cost tens of thousands of dollars to drill a well.

The property was very secluded and the nearest electrical supply was miles away. It was entirely forested with medium growth Ponderosa Pine, Douglas Fir and Western Larch, or Tamarack as it is called in western Montana. The largest of the trees were 12-18 inches at the base so there was potential for building materials and firewood. The only caveat: there was an easement road that ran through the property. It led to a year round occupied log cabin located a twenty minute walk past the property. That later turned out to not be such a big deal.

While walking the property I saw sign of deer and elk and I could see Osprey flying about. The selling agent told us of bears and wolves and stated that it would make an excellent hunting property. The views of the distant mountains were pleasant, and the abundant wildlife and forest had me wanting. My wife felt the same.

That evening we made an offer and it was accepted.

I began the process of cashing in my 401k and we paid for a title search. A few days later we had our land.

The property

WINTER 2012-2013
PLANNING

WE WERE EXCITED but we did not get the title to the land until October and it was too late to start anything out there in the frozen woods. We had to sit out the winter, dreaming and planning. During that time I sold my 2005 Chevy truck for $6,000 and with that cash plus a little left over from the 401k we bought an old diesel pickup truck, a backhoe, an old farm tractor and a post hole digger implement for it. We also purchased a 3,500 watt Duramax generator with electric start.

For $300 I bought a twenty foot shipping container from my good Amish friend Jake, and I delivered it with my beater truck and a borrowed trailer. I planned to use it for lockable tool storage since I would not be staying on site at first.

For Christmas that year my wife gave me a new Husqvarna 460 Rancher chain saw.

I spent time building up my library and reading about permaculture, organic gardening, livestock and construction methods.

My wife and I spent all winter discussing what method we would use to build our house. We talked about stick built, log cabin, slip-form masonry, straw bale, earth berm, underground, and hobbit-like cob houses. A dozen times we would agree on the construction, then a week later we would change our mind. The last idea we agreed upon was the log cabin because we had an abundant supply of logs on the property.

April 2013
Well Pump

THE FIRST ORDER OF BUSINESS was to get the deep well operational.

According to the well report, the well was 520 feet deep and tested at 3.5 gallons per minute. I knew that 500 feet of drop pipe and 8 gauge wire was going to be heavy and I wasn't sure how to go about the process of lowering it into the well casing without some kind of disaster. Before this adventure I also knew almost nothing about wells and how they work. I did know that the steel well casing is pushed into the ground until it reaches bedrock. But how does the water get to the house when it's all underground?

I researched on google and watched a few Youtube videos and I learned what a pitless adapter is. A pitless adapter is a brass fitting in two parts. The bottom part has a threaded nipple that goes through a drilled hole in the side of the well casing from the inside. On the exterior side of the pitless adapter (and the well casing) is where the water line is attached, bringing water to the house. The top half of the pitless adapter screws into the drop pipe, and then is lowered down into the well and slides and locks into the stationary lower half. The lower part of the second half has threads to accept the drop pipe, and the upper part has 1" threads into which you can screw a T-handle made out of regular steel pipe.

To make sure we bought all the right equipment we had consulted with a company in Missoula called Axmen which among other things specializes in farm, ranch, and off grid solutions. Their recommendations matched up with my own research, so from them we purchased a Grundfos SQ Series, 1 HP pump , 500 feet of 1" PVC drop pipe and 8 gauge wire, the pitless adapter, and a few fittings and connectors. (This is also the retailer from which we bought the post hole digger for the tractor and a few other odds and ends.)

I examined my new pitless adapter and saw that I would need to drill a 1-¼" hole into the well casing. The hole must be below the frost depth; otherwise the water in the pipe may freeze in winter.

In early April of 2013 came the first test of the old 1969 Case 480 backhoe that I had bought over the winter for $1,800. It was good to get on a backhoe again. I had once operated a backhoe for a living, and it was like riding a bike for me.

I dug out a 4-½ foot deep pit right up at the well casing. We looked for and found a 1" polypipe that had been buried (but not connected to the well) by a previous land owner. Then we fired up the generator and my wife and I dropped into the pit and with a powerful drill and a good bi-metal hole saw, we cut the 1-¼" hole we needed for the pitless adapter. It took a long time to cut through the ¼" thick well casing.

We then assembled the two halves of the pitless adapter, lowered it into the well with the T-handle and stuck the threaded nipple part through the new hole, towards the outside. Then we installed the rubber washer and screwed the retaining nut onto the outside. I snugged it up good with a pipe wrench.

The next day I drove out to the site and with the backhoe I trenched in about a hundred feet of 4' deep trench. The trench crossed the existing buried polypipe and went to two locations: one for the future camper site and one for the future livestock area. I climbed down into the well hole and connected the polypipe to the pitless adapter. I then went back to where I had trenched across the existing polypipe and cut the original line and added my two new lateral lines with tee adapters. These branches would supply water to some hydrants I was installing.

At the future camper site and the livestock area, I installed the two water hydrants at the other ends of the new polypipe I had just installed. Then I buried everything. I also took the backhoe 300' away to the far end of the existing buried polypipe and installed a hydrant there. This would be the site of the future house. If looked at from above, the final polypipe run resembled a giant Tee, with the well at the top of the Tee, the future house site at the bottom, and the camper and livestock sites at the short legs of the Tee.

I had the piping infrastructure done but we still had to install the well pump.

My wife and I did that a few weeks later with the assistance of her dad, a jolly old Scotsman. It was a lot of work and it took two days to do it. On the ground we laid out 250 feet of the drop pipe and screwed it together. Then I attached it to the pump (along with the wire) and lowered as much of it as I could by hand. That 8 gauge wire added to the weight and I was afraid I was going to drop the whole thing and nick the wire on the edge of the well casing. We tied off the pull string and I parked the backhoe nearby and raised the front bucket. We suspended a big pulley from the bucket. We ran the pull string through the pulley to a car parked some distance away, then we lowered the pump, drop pipe and wire by driving the car slowly toward the well.

After a long stressful day we had the pump lowered about halfway and the Scotsman smiled, rubbing his hands together and said, "I'm surprised everything is going so well!"

Things immediately went to hell. The pull line snapped and the pump started falling. After some panic, we managed to arrest the falling pump and tie it off. Sometimes you just have to quit for awhile and go back another time so that is what we did.

We left it that way for a few days. During that time I built an A-frame over the well so we wouldn't have to use the backhoe to suspend the pulley.

After a few more mishaps, we lowered the well pump down to about 500 feet and screwed the pitless adapter to the top of the last piece of drop pipe. Then we carefully lowered the pitless adapter into its other half, where it held the weight of the whole thing. We immediately powered up the pump with the generator to test it. To my relief we got some good clean water at all three hydrants. The Grundfos SQ pumps have a *soft start* feature, meaning the start-up current is less and they can be run with a smaller generator, but I had been worried.

I was relieved. It was a difficult job and I was glad it was over.

Drilling into the well casing

One of the three water hydrants I installed

The well

APRIL 2013
FIRST FENCING

WE HAD A COUPLE GOATS and a few dozen chickens which were being held temporarily in a very small pen on my in-laws property. I wanted to have the new site fenced in for the animals so that I could move the camper out there and get some serious work done.

In late April the temperatures were perfect for working outside; warm enough to work in a T-shirt, but not too hot. I spent a few days with the backhoe, clearing the perimeter of a rectangle a bit smaller than a football field, where I would put the new fence. The area was partially clear but mostly wooded. I needed to be able to drive the tractor in there to set the posts.

After I cleared the area I began to char the bottoms of the fence posts. My wife and I had determined that we didn't want to use treated posts because of the chemicals used. We felt it was bad for the environment and we thought we might want to start an organic farm someday, and we didn't want the toxic chemicals to cause an issue.

I knew that in the old days people used to char the bottoms of posts to prevent rot but I admit I was not positive the idea would work. I'm not sure what the theory behind the charring is but I do think that post rot happens at the surface level, where tiny organisms thrive and eat. My thinking was that maybe the tiny organisms would not eat the charred wood.

An acquaintance of mine explained it differently: *"The char hardens the surface of the wood and is highly basic(pH), so it helps prevent rot by making the soil immediately around the post inhospitable to detrifiers."*

At any rate I spent a few days charring my fence posts. I would later use this idea while building my cabin.

I spent the next week working the tractor to make holes for the fence posts.

The tractor was a 30 horsepower, gasoline powered 1953 Harry Ferguson TO-30 and it came with a five foot back blade. We had paid $1600 for it the previous winter. We also had gotten a good deal on a new PTO powered post hole digger - the kind with a spinning auger. After digging a few post holes with it I began to realize why so many people died in farm accidents.

I had installed fencing at my previous property so I was familiar with the practice, although I had dug those holes by hand. The hardest part is getting all the posts in a nice straight line. To do this I first dug the holes for the corner posts, set them in and tamped the earth into the holes. I then tied a string low to the ground between two end posts and walked along with a tape measure and a can of ground marking paint and sprayed a circle every ten feet. I then removed the string and drove down the line with the tractor and dug the holes. It is not as easy as it sounds with the type of post hole digger I used because the auger was some distance behind the operator seat, and twisting my head around, I watched it swing back and forth as I lowered it. I tried to time the drop perfectly. But even though it was difficult, it sure was easier than digging the post holes by hand.

For my corner posts I did not use the regular posts we had bought. Instead I cut, peeled, and charred logs of a larger diameter. I used the backhoe to excavate holes and set them four feet into the ground. I learned later that I should have used only tamarack logs because they are more rot resistant, but in this situation I had used both tamarack and douglas fir.

Every corner/end post or gate post needs to be braced; otherwise the tension of the fence will pull the post inward. I used a brace post, spaced eight feet from the corner post, and a horizontal brace pole set about four feet high, which is the height of my fence. My brace poles were 4" tamarack peeled logs. They were pinned into the posts at both ends with a 6" length of 3/8" re bar. I then ran a loop of 10 gauge galvanized solid fence wire diagonally from the bottom of the corner end post to the top of the brace post. I stuck a "twitch stick" into the middle of the loop and turned it until the wire twisted and became very tight. This pulled the top of the brace post back towards the corner post, and the combination of the diagonal wire and the horizontal brace pole made the whole thing very rigid.

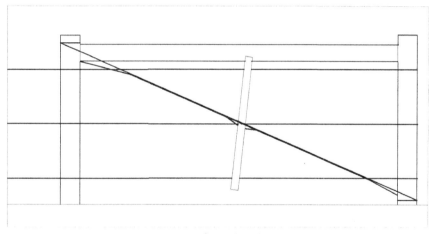

Proper fence bracing

It was during those first few days that I was working on the fencing that I met my only neighbors. The dirt road that runs through the property was an easement road, meaning people have the right to use it to get to their own land.

I was tamping the dirt around a post by the easement road when they drove around the curve in a Land Cruiser and slowed to a stop. They rolled the window down and I stopped working to speak with them for awhile.

They were a married couple in their fifties who lived year-round at a property down the road. From them I learned that there were no other dwellers further down the easement road, so traffic there would be limited to the two of them. There were properties around us but most of the owners lived out of state. He told me about the wolf tracks he had seen earlier and about other wildlife he had seen. He mentioned that he would be glad to keep an eye on my tools and equipment until I moved out to the site.

I could tell right away they were folks just like us who wanted to live free and simply, and we later became good friends.

Charring fence posts

Fence posts along the easement road

MAY 2013
THE CAMPER ARRIVES

IN EARLY MAY OF 2013 I used the backhoe to clear a space for the camper near where I had installed the water hydrant. Then on May 5th, I hooked the camper up to my old diesel truck and pulled it to the site. I took some time parking and leveling the camper, trying my best to make it nice for my wife who would come out a few weeks later. She had decided to stay at her parent's house which was closer to her job while I moved to the site and got things set up.

I had brought the dogs with me. I had a 150 pound Newfoundland called Angus, a female Australian Cattle Dog (in Montana they are called Blue Heelers) named Shiva, and two Jack Russell Terriers; a female named Sugar and a quick little male named Putt-putt. After being penned up in a very small area for the last year or so, they were happy to have space to be free. As I went to sleep that night for the first time at my new land I felt the same way.

Camper fenced in

May 2013
Goats and Chickens

I HADN'T FINISHED THE LIVESTOCK FENCING YET and I spent the next few weeks finishing that up and working on other little projects. By early June I had finished the fence and brought out the goats and chickens. Before I finished with the fencing I had broken the backhoe while digging out a stump in the fence line. The old diesel engine made a horrendous sound and I limped it out of the area and parked it by the well. It was disheartening; we hadn't even begun to build our house yet.

The goats were two mini-Nubian does we had owned for a few years. The plan had been to milk them but we lost the house around the time they became old enough and we just hadn't been able to set things up to do the milking. I was just happy I was able to keep them at my in-laws' place although they were penned up in a very small area and I felt bad for them.

We had about a dozen layer White Rock chickens and a few dozen layer pullets of other breeds we had started raising a few months earlier. In addition we had about 15 Cornish cross meat chickens we were raising for meat.

I threw together a small plywood box for the chickens to sleep in because I didn't want them to get used to roosting in trees at night. I decided the goats would have to rough it in the open for awhile and they didn't seem to mind at all. If it rained they stayed under the thick branches of a fir tree and kept dry. During the day they ate the bark and needles from the abundant firs and tamaracks.

As it turned out I didn't need to give additional feed to the goats all summer; they stayed nice and fat eating the trees and whatever leafy greens they could find. Later I let them out of the fence and let them run loose, day and night. They didn't get eaten by larger predators so I think the presence of the dogs must have kept the wild beasts at bay. The goats never ran away, and they found more leafy greens that way. After my wife came out we often went for walks down the easement road through the woods and the goats always followed us.

Over time I did lose a few chickens. They did not bother staying in the fenced in area during the day and every now and then when I was out walking around I would find a small pile of feathers. I thought it was probably an osprey or eagle that was doing the killing, but I'd only lost two or three that way.

The goats check out their new home

"Will you scratch my ears?"

June 2013
Camper Life

I HAD A FEW PROBLEMS to solve with living in the camper; things people don't normally think about.

We planned to live in the camper while we worked on the land and built a house. It was a fifth wheel trailer and had seen better days. But most of the parts worked and it had running water with tanks, propane fridge and range, and electric lights. The water heater didn't work and I planned to look at it. I had been living in the camper for the last year or two in the backyard of my in-laws so it was like bringing my old home to the new property.

After I had parked the camper I put up about 360 feet of field fence in a rough circle around it. Knowing it was temporary, I stapled the fence to trees and only placed a few posts. The plan was that the fence would keep the chickens out and keep the dogs in. Putt-putt, the male Jack Russell Terrier, liked to kill chickens and the other Jack, a sweet female named Sugar, was older and slightly feeble and would wander off and disappear if given a chance. I put up a gate I had brought from my last property and the fence was good to go.

The chickens eventually started hopping the camper fence and going in to scratch around, thinking the grass was greener over there. So I taught Putt-putt to leave them alone. Jacks are stubborn but very smart.

I had ensured the camper had a supply of water when I had installed the extra water line and the hydrant. I could simply pull the generator out to the well (a distance of about 150 feet), connect a hose to the hydrant, and fill up the 30 gallon tank in the camper. When all four of us were there and if we did a load of laundry every day we used about one 30 gallon tank per day, which meant we had to fill the tank once per day.

The washing machine was a newer model we had brought from the old house. I parked it outside the camper and ran water lines from the camper to it. I also ran discharge line to a drain on the ground about 20 feet away. We dried our clothes the old fashioned way; hanging them outside on a line. This method of doing laundry would work until we got freezing temperatures.

After my wife came out to the camper to stay with me in late June we took solar hot showers. We hung a plastic water bag on a tree and let the sun heat it up. The bag had a little shower spout on it. I had hung a shower curtain around it and it worked okay, but a better base to stand on would have been nice; the twigs poked me in my feet. After I showered I would walk naked to a lawn chair and dry in the sun. There was no one to see except the dogs and a few squirrels and my wife, who was more modest and thought I was crazy.

Later, after the kids came out for the summer, I fixed the hot water heater so we could shower in the camper and morale improved.

JUNE 2013
CHICKEN COOP

IN MID-JUNE I started work on the chicken coop. It took longer than I thought it would to finish it because although I had done a lot of reading, I had no experience in building with logs.

I had decided to build the coop as a small log cabin with coped notches at the corners. It looked simple enough, and my thinking was that I would probably build our home that way and building the coop would be good practice.

I thought about the foundation for awhile, then I shrugged and decided I would do it the way the pioneers did it. I found four large flat rocks and arranged them on the ground in a rectangle about sixteen feet by ten feet. I had tried to dig out the sod first, but I didn't put much effort into it. On these rocks I would place my first two logs.

I spent the next few days cutting down trees, dragging them to the coop and peeling them to turn them into pretty cabin logs. I used an old fashioned draw knife for most of the peeling, but at times I used a regular hatchet. By this time I had learned that tamarack logs peeled easier than fir, and they seemed to grow nice and straight so tamarack is what I used for most of the logs in the coop. It was later that I learned about the rot-resistance of that species, so it seems that I lucked out.

By this time, towards the end of June, the sun was out and it was starting to get hot during the day. Later in the summer the temperatures would go over a hundred degrees, and peeling logs in the sun is a tiring chore. Sometimes I would peel the logs where they fell if it was in a shady area. As always, Angus and Shiva were with me on these trips out into the woods. Shiva learned to run away whenever she heard the chain saw engine, but I had to constantly watch out for Angus to make sure I didn't drop a tree on my big goofy pal.

I didn't cut and peel all the logs in one big bunch because peeling logs is tedious work, especially when it's hot. So I would cut and peel a few and stage them with the tractor, then work on cutting the notches and placing them.

For the first two logs I cut a flat spot at each end with the chain saw, then maneuvered them into position so that the flat notches sat on the rocks. To cut the notches, I would first mark it with a Sharpie, then cut grooves about an inch apart from one another. Then I would pound those out with a hammer and run the saw into the notch to give it a flat surface. Making flat notches was fairly easy.

On the next two logs I had to make a coped notch, which is shaped to fit over the round log beneath it. I first placed the whole log into position, then set a compass at half the diameter of the lower log. Then with the pointy end of the compass riding along the lower log, I marked a semicircular line on the upper log. (They make a professional version of this tool called a "log scribe" but they're very pricey and I didn't have one. If I was going to build a house this way I would buy the tool.) I then rolled the log onto its top and used the same technique I had used to make the flat notches. Those cope notches had to be perfect or there were gaps. Usually I had to do two or three modifications to the notch, rolling the log around each time. Making coped notches that fit well was harder I thought it would be. I decided if I ever build another log cabin, I would use a different method of joining logs.

On the first two rows of logs I drilled ½" holes through the corners and pounded in re bar to bind the two logs tightly.

The upper parts of the walls went in the same way, although it took two months to finish them with the help of my wife, son and daughter. They did a lot of the work, peeling logs and helping me get them into position. Some of the upper logs were difficult to get into position. The highest part of the wall was just over my head, and the logs were green, felled only the day before, and very heavy. There was nowhere to hang my come-along, so I lifted them up with brute strength. Over that summer I lost some fat and gained some muscle. I was 47 years old at the time so I was careful not to hurt my back, but I did get a workout.

It was hot sweaty work and we took a lot of breaks in the camper, where it was just as hot, but at least the sun didn't shine on us. The camper was poorly insulated and the inside temperature on those days was over a hundred degrees. We just sat on the furniture, sweating and gulping water, with little fans pointed at us.

I installed two small windows which we had bought at the local home re-use store for five dollars each. Before I put them in I had to attach boards to the inside of the window opening and I cut those boards out of a ponderosa pine log with my chainsaw mill. This was the first time I used the chainsaw mill and it did a fine job, although it took awhile to set up. I also cut the boards for the door frame and for the vertical wall and ceiling for the goat shelter.

I put re bar pins in at the door and window openings and at the corners of the top logs. I decided to build a half-height wall inside about two thirds of the way down the length of the coop. This smaller section would be where the goats could shelter and I planned to put nesting boxes above it.

In early August we began work on the roof of the coop. We cut and peeled ten logs roughly 4"-6" in diameter to serve as rafters and pinned five of them to the long walls with re bar. The other logs were bolted perpendicular to tops of the rafters to serve as girders to support the steel roofing. For bolts we used 3/8" threaded rod (all-thread) and washers and nuts. I drilled holes and pounded the rods through and we tightened them up. I worked from the roof and my wife worked from the ground and together we made a good team.

Finally on August 16th we put on the metal roofing we had been saving. We had brought the roofing from the old property and although the colors were mismatched, it worked perfectly.

I cut a sapling and mounted it inside for a roost and we lined the floor with straw. That evening we chased the chickens for an hour and locked them up inside. From that night on they went into the coop on their own when the sun set. We felt good. The chickens and goats had a shelter for the winter.

But we couldn't help thinking about our own home which we had yet to build. The backhoe was broken, we had very little money, and winter was only a few months away.

Tina peeling a log

Troy helps out

First row of logs

Drilling holes for re bar pins

Walls going up!

Chainsaw-cut boards

Five dollar window

Haleigh peels a log for the roof

Starting the roof

Finished Coop

SUMMER 2013
GREY WATER

OUR CAMPER was set up in the middle of the woods, with no electric, water, or sewer hookups. I had solved the water supply problem, and we ran a generator to recharge the camper batteries, but I had to come up with an environmentally safe way to deal with the sewer.

The first spring when I lived alone in the camper it wasn't a problem. A man can pee outside and its no big deal. And backpackers learn what to do with the other thing, which is what I did. I simply dug a hole, did my business in it, and filled in the hole with earth.

I needed a longer term solution for when my wife and kids came out to stay. My wife was definitely not going to poop in a hole in the ground!

Before we bought the land, when I had lots of time to read, one of the many books I read was *Create an Oasis with Greywater* by Art Ludwig. I consider this the defacto guide book to grey water discharge systems. Art is a pioneer; at the time I read the book it was the only available book on the subject and I encourage anyone considering installing a grey water system to read both Art's web site and his book. His web site is at http://oasisdesign.net and the book is available there for purchase.

According to Art's web site the benefits of grey water recycling are:

- Lower fresh water use
- Less strain on septic tank or treatment plant
- Highly effective purification
- Site unsuitable for a septic tank
- Less energy and chemical use
- Groundwater recharge
- Plant growth
- Reclamation of otherwise wasted nutrients
- Increased awareness of and sensitivity to natural cycles

In a nutshell, grey water systems direct used water from the sinks, laundry, and shower to a wood mulch pit with a tree or other beneficial plant growing in the center of the pit, on a raised mound. (Laws vary by state as far as what particular water can be directed to grey water reuse.) The high carbon material of the wood mulch breaks down the stinky part of the grey water, and at the same time the tree gets irrigated.

In the more hard-core systems outlined in Art's book, he suggests that toilet water can be directed to the grey water system as long as no one defecates in the toilet. If solid human waste is added to the grey water you no longer have grey water; you have *black water*. Black water is toxic, really gross and bad for the environment. So I had to think of a solution for that hurdle and I'll come to it in a bit.

I didn't have time or a good reason to build up a fancy grey water system for the camper. I just needed a way to get all the grey water to be disposed of safely.

I dug a hole 2 foot deep by 2 foot wide. I didn't have wood chips but I had plenty of tree bark after building the log cabin chicken coop. I ran a short PVC pipe from the camper drain to the hole. Then I covered it up with the top part of a 55 gallon blue water drum. I sealed all cracks with dirt and crumpled up a fir branch and stuck it in the hole on the drum to act as a screened vent. After about a month there was no smell, even if I pulled the branch out and took a big sniff.

Later after four of us were living in the camper we could sometimes detect an odor from the hole. At that point, my small pit was probably overloaded.

The other part of my solution was an outhouse with a composting toilet inside. The idea is that of a simple small room with walls and a floor. On the floor is a 5 gallon bucket in a plywood box with a hole cut in the top. A regular toilet seat is attached over the hole. You do your business in the bucket, then cover it with wood chips or sawdust. When the bucket is full, empty it into a compost pile.

To build the outhouse I mostly used my preferred source of materials - stuff I had lying around. I didn't get it finished until late fall, and by that time my son was the the only other person with me. The first thing he did was add a shower curtain in the doorway. I was quite happy without a door; the view was great!

There are many sources which say that "humanure" composted this way is perfectly safe and acceptable to be used as compost for food producing plants, as long as there are no people on medication using the bucket.

Probably the most famous resource for researching this concept is *The Humanure Handbook* by Joseph Jenkins, available at http://humanurehandbook.com/.

In the future we may build a real septic system but for now the grey water system and outhouse are working great. Later in the book I will discuss the grey water system I built for the cabin.

Grey water pit

Outhouse construction

All it needs is a door!

Summer 2013
Backhoe Repairs

IN THE WEEKS AFTER we finished the chicken coop, my wife and I worked on the backhoe. It was a frustrating job and the machine was parked in direct sunlight and it couldn't be moved. We were dirty and greasy and hot. I accidentally left a Gerber knife when I left to take a break and when I returned I found that glue that holds the rubber grip had melted away. We found that we had to remove a dozen parts to get to where we could see one of the dozens of parts we needed to remove in order to get to the engine. And every part was in a blind spot and hard to get to, and coated in grease.

It was around this time that the white and brown goat drank some motor oil out of a bucket that I had left by the backhoe. We knew what she had done because we could see the oil around her lips. She was sick for days and laid around moaning and made some interesting poop, and I thought she was going to die. I felt awful for leaving that bucket where she could find it. I couldn't really tell how much oil the poor girl drank cause it was a 5 gallon bucket that was part motor oil, part hydraulic oil, and part antifreeze that I had drained out of the backhoe.

I thought with the antifreeze she surely would die a painful death. My wife looked it up on the internet and as we already knew, there is nothing you can do about it. So taking the goat to the vet wouldn't help. For three days the poor goat would not eat or drink and would just lay on the ground moaning, sounding just like a person who was in a lot of pain would sound like.

I hate to see animals suffer and I considered shooting her, but I decided to let it play out and she lived. I learned my lesson about leaving toxic goop lying around. I was very glad I didn't have to shoot her; I don't know if I could have done it.

I cleaned up the area around the backhoe and got back to work on it. I've never worked as a mechanic, but in my younger years I liked to hot rod cars. I once built a Chevy small block engine with a bare block I had bought at a junkyard and with mail order parts, so I was familiar with working on engines. But that old Case was difficult. I already owned most of the tools I needed, but I had to buy a giant sized wrench set they sell at Harbor Freight and also a few other tools.

Eventually I removed the cylinder head. I celebrated because it took me three days to do it. Then I removed the oil pan and tapped out the pistons one at a time so I could get a good look at the crankshaft, which is where the problem turned out to be; the crankshaft was broken into two pieces.

I fooled around for awhile trying to get the engine block out, but there was not enough clearance underneath to drag it out and I had no way to hoist it up over the top. I was thinking about solutions for that, but the reason I suspended work on it was because we had shopped around and the least expensive replacement crankshaft we could find was a used one at $600. We never did seem to have that much money at one time so we just let it be for awhile.

That was a year and a half ago. We still talk about getting the old backhoe up and running. At some point we'll do it, but there always seems to be other priorities.

FALL 2013
WINTER IS COMING

D URING THE FALL OF 2013, my wife and I discussed our situation. We didn't have a house to live in and the camper was not winter-proof, which means the water lines would freeze in the cold. That was no place for a 15 year old girl to live, unable to take a shower before school! So we decided that my wife and daughter would return to the in-laws' house for the school year and the winter. Our son was taking a break from college and he would stay with me in the camper and help me with whatever needed doing.

What needed doing was taking care of the animals, including the dogs, and keeping the inside of the camper warm enough to keep us from freezing to death. As it turned out it also meant doing some heavy construction work outside in the freezing cold all winter long.

I made preparations for winter. I put the small wood stove back into the camper. I had bought it the winter before at Harbor Freight for $90. It was a box wood style stove with round removable covers on top so a person could set pots on it to cook.

I had put a heat shield on the wall behind the stove. Underneath was a raised platform of two layers of fiber cement board with an air gap underneath. I used double wall stove pipe and a proper ceiling adapter through the skylight opening in the ceiling, and used triple wall pipe outside. Even when the stove got red hot, the floor below and the wall behind remained cool.

Caution: Running a wood stove in a camper is not recommended and is probably illegal everywhere! A camper is like a tinder box, and will completely engulf in seconds! People die in all the time in camper fires!

I placed straw bales around the perimeter of the camper to keep cold wind out, and I put heat tape on all the water lines so that when the generator was running they wouldn't freeze. Later when it got cold they froze anyway.

I built a small wood shed and spent some time looking for standing dead trees. I felled and dragged them to the new wood shed. I built up a nice pile of firewood under the shed and I felt pleased with myself, and I found out later that it was not nearly enough. It was to be a long, cold winter.

My daughter left in late August and my wife planned to leave at a later date. We discussed the future of our housing situation. At length we came up with a plan to start work on a temporary cabin, which we would live in and then take our time building our dream home.

It sounded simple enough. My wife said, "Maybe we can get it done by Christmas?"

Remembering how long it had taken me to build the chicken coop, I tried not to burst out laughing. But I was motivated, so we agreed to begin.

Boxwood Stove

Rustic Woodshed

PART THREE
THE CABIN

Fall 2013
Plans for a Cabin

THE DESIGN WE AGREED UPON for the temporary cabin was that of a pole barn style building, with posts set in the ground and a crawl space under the floor. The posts would be peeled and the bottoms charred, and I spent some time working with AutoCAD and Revit Architecture and came up with a floor plan and dimensions.

It would be a simple rectangle, 32 feet by 24 feet, oriented east-west, and have a steel roof to collect rainwater. The posts would be notched to hold beams or girders, and the floor joists would rest on the beams. At the top there would be a ridge pole, two purlin poles, and two eave poles. We would set the 2x4 walls on the flooring. Inside the cabin there would be two bedrooms, a combined living room/kitchen, a mudroom, a pantry, and a bathroom.

It was October and soon the ground would soon freeze so I felt we had to get moving. We picked a site and started digging holes.

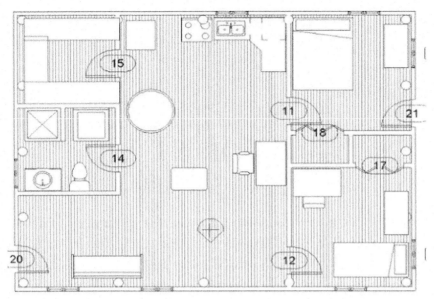

Floor plan

Fall 2013
Cabin Posts

BEFORE I COULD START DIGGING I had to remove two giant ponderosa pines that were in the way. I was an amateur at felling trees, and my 20 foot tool container was in a dangerous location. I spent a long time planning my cuts, and in the end they both fell right where I wanted them to.

I dragged them out of the way with the tractor, and we pounded stakes at the corners, running a string and using the 3-4-5 method to check for squareness. Then we measured the diagonals and adjusted the stakes as needed. Then we tied a string around the perimeter of the four stakes, and with a tape measure and marking paint we marked the holes.

I used the post hole digger on the tractor but it was quickly obvious that the auger was too small. I knew we were going to use 10"-12" posts so I ended up digging them all by hand. There were 18 holes altogether and it took me a few days.

I spent the next few days felling trees and dragging them to the site. I did not bring over all 18 logs at once because I didn't have room to lay them all out.

We had purchased a tool called the Log Wizard in hopes of speeding up the bark peeling process. It is essentially a planer that can be attached to the end of a chainsaw and driven by a regular (although a bit longer) chain. I put it on my smaller chainsaw and once I got the hang of it, it did a good job but it was a bear to work with. If I held the tool too low it cut into the wood too much.

The center of balance was awkward so that holding it in the right position was difficult. I would do one log and then take a break because working with a chainsaw while exhausted is not a good idea. In fact, during one of those breaks I happened to notice a cut on the leg area in the outer layer of my Carhart bibs. I had let the running chain get to close to my leg and not noticed. I had come within an eighth inch of a serious hospital visit.

On November 13th I began charring the bottoms of the posts I had peeled. It took me all day to char nine logs because it was raining and everything was damp.

The next day my wife and I began setting the posts. Setting a 20 foot green post with a tractor and a come-along was hard work. I took the auger off the post hole digger and used the boom on the implement to move the post to position. We stuck a board in the hole to keep the post from digging in the dirt. Then we lifted the top end of the post up about 6 feet and rested it on cross beams, with the bottom of the post at the edge of the hole. Then I moved the tractor to the opposite side of the hole, raise the boom on the implement, and used a come-along to crank the post toward vertical. It took us a little while to work out the system, but once we got it figured out it went along quickly, although it was still a lot of physical work.

By the 18th the rain had turned to snow but we had all eighteen posts set and ready to go. The next step was to get the roof purlins up on top but I didn't get much done for the next month or so. I had some paid work come in that I had to do, and then Christmas arrived.

Using the Log Wizard

Charring posts in the rain

Preparing to hoist the post up into the air

Lifting the posts

Leveling and tamping

Almost halfway done

Finally done with the posts!

WINTER 2013
IN THE COLD

BY EARLY JANUARY my wife had moved to the in-laws house for the winter, and my seventeen year old son was staying with me over the winter in the camper.

It was a good thing my wife left because it was a cold, snowy winter. Before it was over we saw outside temperatures as low as twenty-five below zero and at least four feet of snow. My old truck had a rebellious diesel engine and most of the time if I wanted to bring it to life I had to drag the generator out to the truck, plug in the block heater, and heat up the engine block for 45 minutes. Sometimes that generator didn't want to start; it was an electric start and the pull cord had broken off some time ago. On those really cold mornings the battery was too weak to start the little generator engine and I had to use an extra battery from the camper to jump start it.

The camper was not well insulated and I could not keep the water lines from freezing so our supply of water was three or four 5 gallon jugs. We didn't have room for all of them in the camper so we kept them outside where they froze solid after a few minutes. We kept one jug in the camper by the stove to keep it halfway thawed out. From this single jug we obtained water for washing and cooking and this is also where we got water for the dogs and livestock. If we wanted to shower we drove to the in-laws' house, where I also filled the water jugs. It was an hour drive so we made the trip once a week or sometimes every two weeks. I didn't take the truck out very often to go to the store either because the mountain road was deep with snow and my four-wheel-drive truck with summer tires would sometimes get stuck and I would have to dig it out with a shovel.

The morning temperatures in the camper were sometimes as low as ten degrees but we had thick blankets to sleep with and dogs to keep us warm. The little boxwood stove would not hold a fire all night no matter how much wood we stuffed into it, so every morning the dog's water bowl and the water jug were frozen solid.

I always made sure I had a supply of kindling and firewood ready before bed. In the mornings I spent the first freezing minutes of the day coaxing a fire into life, offering my hands to beg it's warmth. Then I would get some water from the refrigerator (I kept some water in the fridge to keep it from freezing!) and set a kettle on the stove. I'd also put on a pot of water to make oatmeal, and I would sit in the chair with my heavy coat on waiting for the place to warm up and for the water jug to thaw out.

If we didn't have a lot to do I spent most of my time reading by the fire or surfing the internet over my cell phone connection. In the evening we would turn on the satellite TV and I watched "The Five" on Fox News, especially after a day of working outside. Then at night we sometimes watched a Netflix show.

The daily chores didn't add up to much on the days we weren't working on the cabin. The first thing we would do was get the livestock some water. We filled a 3 gallon pail from the jug and carried it out to them, but there was no way to keep it from freezing. On the coldest days after only three or four minutes the water in the bucket was slushy like a frozen margarita. I felt bad for the animals, especially the goats, and I fed them some extra corn. We had rabbits at that time, and I kept their cage full of straw and put a thick blanket over it, but one of them died, anyway. I don't know if it died from the cold, but the other rabbit lived for another year so maybe it was just old age that got her.

I never did get the chicken coop sealed up as well as I wanted and it was drafty. I had sealed up all the cracks with expanding foam but the darn chickens pecked at it wherever they could reach it until there were holes again. The goats ate it, too. But despite the subzero temperatures, we didn't lose any chickens or goats. I can't help but think how tough those animals are surviving out there in that cold.

For awhile it seemed like every night a foot of snow was dumped on us. Every morning, especially if we were working on the cabin, I would spend some time getting the tractor started and plow the night's snow out of the driveway and the area we were working in, and also out to the well so we could drag the generator out there if we needed to. My son shoveled the snow in the animal pen so that we could walk around in there and have a place to throw the chicken feed. Some days I would take the tractor out and look for some more firewood, dead standing trees that I could cut down and drag back to the camper. I tried to put off wood gathering until the days when the temperature was up in the twenties.

One thing I learned about the really cold days is that the sun shone really brightly and we got some good solar charging voltage. But it didn't last long because the sun came up from behind the east mountains at ten o'clock and went behind the west mountains at around three o'clock.

Twice during the winter a distant neighbor plowed the whole easement road with his big diesel tractor on tracks. Both times the snow in the road was two or three feet deep. Ron was a retired Vietnam veteran and he didn't even know I was living out there until I heard his tractor and ran over to see what was going on. He was plowing the road mostly for the neighbors who lived down the easement road. I was glad he did the plowing and I tried to give him some money for diesel fuel but he wouldn't take it.

Those days we often didn't have a lot of money for gas for the generator so we would only run it two or three hours a day. We could make a five gallon can of gas last a week.

In January I had started working on the cabin again, with my son helping me. I knew my wife was looking forward to getting the cabin done because she was also going a little crazy living with her parents. The cabin was a long way from getting finished, but I wasn't getting any paid work and I felt like I had to work on something productive.

While working on the cabin that winter I had to do a lot of work on ladders. My son suffered from acrophobia but he did anything I asked him to do if it didn't require climbing a ladder. He did a lot of dragging around chains and ropes and tossing up tools to me while I was on the ladder. He turned his back when I did some of the more scary work, like operating the chainsaw above my head while standing on top of a ten foot step ladder with nothing to hang onto. He said couldn't watch because it made him sick to his stomach. I honestly didn't feel too good about it either.

The working conditions were tough; freezing cold and constant struggling with the deep snow, looking for buried tools or working with frozen ropes. Sometimes we had to take breaks to thaw out and dry our gloves and boots by the stove. During these breaks and after quitting for the day I would try to plan out our next operation. I found that sometimes I spent more time planning how to do things than I did actually doing the things.

My son and I both went a little crazy I think, living and working so close together all winter in that tough situation. We had no way to get away from each other - we either worked together outside or were stuck together in the camper. We got to know each other a little too well. Considering our circumstances I think we did pretty well, but we did argue a few times and by the time spring arrived I didn't know whether I was glad to have him there to help me or if I wanted to kick him out!

But for the most part he kept up a good attitude and we managed to joke around and laugh about how difficult everything was. Since then, when it gets cold, I think about how my son and I survived for those winter months in that frigid camper and about how proud of him I was.

Winter on the homestead

.

January 2014
Cabin Purlins

IN THE FIRST MONTH OF THE NEW YEAR my son and I began work on the next phase of the cabin, which was to get the ridge pole and four purlins installed. These are the long heavy poles that span the long length of the roof, supporting the rafters above. I planned to space the purlins about seven feet apart so that the rafter span would be fairly short. At such a short span I could use 2x6 rafters to support the roof and the heavy snow load.

I had drawn up the plans in AutoCAD 3D, so I knew exactly at what height the poles needed to be set on top of the posts. So the first step was to cut all the posts at the right height. This can be tricky to do on uneven terrain - you can't simply hold a tape measure on the post and measure from the ground; the tops will not be level with each other. And I did not own a fancy laser transit.

Before the temperature had dropped below freezing we had marked a reference line on each post with a water level.

We had partially filled a long transparent hose with blue Kool-aid and removed all air bubbles. Then we drew an arbitrary horizontal reference line on one of the center posts a couple feet off the ground. Because this first line was only a reference mark the exact height wasn't important.

Then, my son held the hose up to the reference mark so that he could see that the water level was dead even with the line. While he kept a steady eye on his water level to make sure it didn't move, I held the other end of the hose and matched the water level to each additional post and marked a matching horizontal reference line. This took quite awhile because moving the hose around sloshes the fluid and if not careful, air bubbles can get inside and it screws up the whole thing. But when we were done we had a good reference line on every post and they were all level with each other.

From there I climbed a ladder at each post and lowered a tape measure. While my son held the tape measure on the reference mark, I marked the top of the post where it needed to be cut, and then I cut it off with a chainsaw.

We cut and peeled five logs to serve as purlins; about 10-12" in diameter at the big end and about forty feet long. They were live tamarack trees when I felled them and I don't know how to estimate their weight, but I feel pretty confident in saying they must have each weighed around a ton.

The posts that support the center ridgepole were the tallest, at about 16-½ feet from the ground. The shortest posts on the eave sides of the cabin were about 10-½ feet tall. When I first started this project I didn't have any idea how I was going to get those purlins up there on top of the posts.

Earlier, I had tried for weeks to figure out a way to do it. My son asked me a few times what we were going to do. I told him I had a plan, although I didn't really. I would go to sleep thinking about it and wake up thinking about it. I finally came up with an idea but wasn't sure it was going to work. I hadn't thought of any other ideas by the time I cut the top off every post, so I explained my idea to my son. He laughed and thought I was going senile. But we had no other choice so we did it.

We started with the lowest purlins first, which would be set on the 10-½ foot tall posts along the outsides of the cabin. We dragged the first 40 foot long purlin to lay alongside the eave posts. We measured and cut flat notches on the purlin so it would have a good stable fit on the posts after we got it up there. I then drilled a ½" hole all the way through the log at each flat notch.

Getting The Lifting Poles Into Position

The plan was to attach a temporary "lifting pole" to a corner post, then hang a pulley from the top of the lifting pole. Then we would repeat the process on the other corner post. With the pulley in place we could hoist up the purlin, one end at a time. But getting to that point was a lot of work and took a long time.

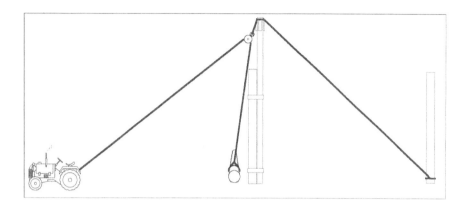

Posts, lifting pole, and anchor line

We spent a day setting up the two lifting poles. It took the whole day to figure out the process, explain it to my son, make the poles and get them into position. At the end of the day we hadn't even started to get the purlin up. The lifting poles were too heavy to get in place by hand; we had to use the tractor to pull up the top end of each one so that it would be higher than the post. The way they moved around when hoisting them into place was dangerous. Our stress level was high and the dogs sensed it. We had to constantly get them out of the way because I was afraid they would get killed. In fact, it seemed like as soon as I climbed on the tractor to lift a heavy log, big goofy Angus would lie down as if to take a nap right in the spot where the log might fall. My son had to run in and kick him out every time. I could have locked him up, but Angus' favorite time of the day was when he went out to work with us and I didn't have the heart to lock him up, so we dealt with it.

To make a lifting pole we cut a straight log about 20 feet long and about 7 or 8 inches in diameter at the big end. We dragged it to a corner post so that the big end of the lifting pole was at the base of the post. We tied the big end of the lifting pole loosely to the corner post to hold it in place. I nailed four 2x4 scraps to the small end of the lifting pole; this would be the top of it. At the top of the corner post I nailed a couple 2x4 scraps (like I had done on the lifting pole) so that I could hang a chain on the post and keep it from sliding down. Then I hung a stout pulley from the chain. So we had the pulley hanging from the top of the corner post. We ran a 100' rope through the pulley and back down and tied one end to the old Harry Ferguson tractor and the other end to the top of the lifting pole. I climbed on the tractor, my son stood well away from the whole thing, and using the tractor and the rope, I pulled the lifting pole up vertical so it was standing next to the post.

Leaving tension on the rope, I shut off the tractor and wrapped a 3" wide cargo tie-down strap around the lower part of the post and lifting pole together and cinched it down tight. I then climbed the ladder and put another tie-down strap around the post and lifting pole together near the top, so the lifting pole was tightly held against the post and they were right beside one another, with the lifting pole being much taller. I took down the rope, chain and pulley. At this point all we had accomplished was to get one lifting pole into position and it had taken hours to get that far.

Then leaving the lifting pole fastened to the post, we did the same thing with a second lifting pole at the opposite corner post and cinched it down tight with the cargo straps. At this point we had two lifting poles in place (one at either end of the cabin) and we were ready to start hoisting the first purlin into place. But it was getting late and we stopped for the day.

So the first day we got the lifting poles into position, and the next day we actually worked on getting the first purlin lifted up into place.

Hoisting the Purlins

The plan was to use the rope, the tractor and the pulley (hanging from the top of the lifting pole) to pull the purlin up. First we would lift one end, then secure the purlin to the top of the post with a rope. Then we would move the pulley to the other lifting pole at the other end, and hoist up the other end of the purlin.

I was afraid the tension of the rope while hoisting up the purlin would topple the corner post and lifting pole to the ground. So before we lifted the purlin we had to brace the lifting pole. We did this by attaching an anchor rope from the top of the lifting pole and running it to the bottom of another post, opposite of the direction in which I was going to drive the tractor. (This is similar to a fencing brace post.) We cinched that anchor rope down tight with the come-along. As I drove the tractor, it tried to pull the top of the lifting pole over but couldn't because it was anchored to the bottom of a different post.

After we were set up it took only a few minutes to get that first purlin up into place. My son was genuinely impressed. We had ran the rope through the pulley at the top of the lifting pole, tied one end to the purlin and the other end to the tractor and it hoisted right up (after we moved the dog, of course.) Then we moved the pulley to the lifting pole at the other end of the purlin and lifted that end up.

As hard as I tried I never managed to get the purlin in place so that the flat notches faced "down" toward the post. I always needed to rotate the purlin after it was in place. I did this by nailing a 2x4 scrap to the purlin, then looping a chain around the 2x4, I then wrapped the chain around the purlin a few times. The other end of the chain was hooked to a come-along hanging from the top of the lifting pole. As I cranked the come-along, the log rotated until the flat notches hit the the bottom and the purlin dropped into place.

Once that was done, while the purlin was still tied to the lifting poles, I climbed up with my big drill and drilled through the holes I had previously put into the purlin. I drilled right into the posts a good 16" or so. Then with a 3 lb hammer I pounded re-bar all the way into the purlin and post to pin them together.

Then we deconstructed the lifting poles and moved them the next purlin to be lifted. By the time we had lifted up all four purlins and the ridge pole, we were getting good enough that we could almost lift one from start to finish in a single day.

I didn't have a tall enough step ladder to allow me to stand on it and hold a drill to put the re-bar spike in the ridge pole. I built some rickety scaffolding out of 2x4s and laid some boards across. I was only 16 feet in the air but it seemed a lot higher from up there.

By the beginning of February we had finished getting the purlins in place.

The eave purlins are installed

Only the ridgepole is left to install

January 2014
Cabin Roof

B Y MID-FEBRUARY we had saved enough money to buy rafters. They were 16' long 2x6 boards which would provide a two foot overhang at the eave. I showed my son how to use the speed square to mark the angles on the top ends of the rafters and he set to work with the hand saw. I worked from the ladder while he handed me rafters and I toenailed them into the purlins. I learned that when toenailing on the very end of the rafter it was better to pre-drill the hole or the nail would split the wood.

We were still in the throes of winter at that time and I had to use a broom to push the snow off the purlins before I could set the rafters up there.

Due to the varying natural taper of the purlins, the rafters did not sit perfectly on all three poles but it was very close. I had to saw some notches in the center purlin to get the rafters to sit down flush but considering the nature of the work we had done, with posts in the dirt and no concrete foundation to work with, and the taper of logs, I was surprised it worked out so well. But sawing those purlin notches with the chainsaw while standing on top of the ten foot step ladder was another one of those harrowing experiences and I was glad to be done with it.

February 21st we put up the last rafter and I had a smile on my face. I felt as if we had surpassed a milestone. I then spent a few days nailing a steel rafter tie plate at three points along each rafter; the ridgepole and each purlin.

After that the plan was to nail 1x4s spaced every 18 inches on top of and perpendicular to the rafters. Then on top of the 1x4s would go the steel roofing.

I thought for a long time about putting a moisture barrier such as tar paper down under the metal, and I considered all the metal roofed sheds I have owned and that I have seen. But I never saw any water leaking through a metal roof unless it was rusted through or had big holes in it.

I try to follow accepted standards and practices whenever I can, for safety reasons and to prolong the life of the building materials I use. But I couldn't figure out why I needed to use that tar paper! I've had pole barns in the past and they never leaked in a way that tar paper would help with. I thought if the metal roofing is installed correctly, with the correct roofing screws and with no unsealed holes (sometimes you goof and poke a hole in the wrong place) it will not pass water to the rafters.

Later I did more research on the need for a moisture barrier on the roof. From what I can tell, it is to help in the event of condensation on the underside of the roof if there is an ice dam built up on the eave. According to what I have read in my building books it is best to avoid this condensation potential altogether and with proper ventilation there should be no ice dams or condensation. The rafters are 2x6 (1.5"x5.5" actual) and for the rafters that have insulation it will be 4" fiberglass insulation (I planned to add rigid styrofoam insulation underneath the rafters) to leave a 1.5" air gap at the top (between the metal roof and the insulation) for passive ventilation. With the ventilation there supposedly should be no ice dam buildup which leads to condensation. At any rate, I decided to keep an eye on it and if it became a problem I would re-do some things. After everything I have done so far it would not be catastrophic if I need to pull the roof panels off and add some underlayment.

Construction slowed while we saved up money for hundreds of feet of 1x4 boards. We were paying cash for materials as we went along and we had to wait for my wife's check and at the same time pay bills and buy groceries and raise a fifteen year old girl and feed my son. I took that time to catch up on chores, gather more firewood, and read.

We didn't get the boards until some time in March and the weather had started turning toward spring by that time. When the temperature reached the thirties we started wearing T-shirts outside and my son walked around outside in basketball shorts. It was like a heat wave to us; we were used to the sub-zero cold for so long.

Once we got the boards, we brought the generator and the air compressor to the cabin so I could use the nail gun up on the roof. I called out measurements from the roof and my son cut the boards on a miter saw and handed them up. We put the 1x4s up in just a few days and I was excited because the construction was really starting to look like a house.

Then we had to save up $750 for the steel roofing panels and it took a long time. That was the largest single expense yet for our new cabin.

Montana Homestead

Rafters installed

It's looking like a cabin!

Spring 2014
Floor

I N THE MEAN TIME I was thinking about what I could get done to make progress on the cabin. I thought about ideas for the floor and decided that I would cut notches in the posts and set girders in the notches. I had never read about it being done but I also couldn't find any reason why it should not work. Except what if the girders shrank or moved or otherwise somehow fell out of the notches? Then the whole floor would collapse and it would be a disaster. I tried to think about a better way to support the girders, but I didn't want to cut into the posts too much and weaken them. I am not an experienced timber framer by any means, and even if I was, I didn't think that would fit into that category.

My plan would give me a girder spacing of 6-½ feet, and on top of the girders I would set the floor joists. This way the span for the joists would be only 6-½ feet, and I could use a smaller joist to support a greater amount of weight. My construction books indicated I could use a 2x6 joist and I decided it was a good idea. I briefly looked at tables for girder sizes and found that a 4x7 girder would be strong enough to support the floor joists.

Before we installed any girders we used the water level to make a mark on each post where the top of each girder should be. I tried to plan the mark so that after the girders, the joists and the sub-floor were in I could use stud-length 2x4s in the exterior walls, with a single bottom plate nailed to the floor, and single top plate nailed to the eave purlins. I was off a little bit due to a math error, but it all worked out in the end.

The girders I needed were very expensive and I didn't have money to buy them. I needed 14 girders roughly 7 feet long and 3 girders (in the center of the house) roughly 14 feet long. I decided I would to use my chain saw mill to make the 17 girders myself. The chain saw mill works very well for making beams. It still takes a long time and if I didn't take a lot of time to set things up the girders weren't real pretty, but it did the job.

Most of the girders I made were bigger than 4x7; I simply made the thickest girder I could from every log that I used. On some of them I used the chain saw mill to cut one flat surface and then peeled off the rest of the bark and left the girder mostly round. The 14 foot long girders were done this way and were extra thick and heavy.

My son and I started mounting the girders. I cut notches in the posts and after measuring the distance and cutting the girder to length we put the beam in place with the help of a sledge hammer. I spiked the girders in place with a 6" steel spike.

After thinking about it for a long time, I decided that the girders were never going to shrink enough or move enough to fall out of the notches in the posts. But I came up with a plan for just in case. I thought back to how I had supported the chicken coop on flat rocks and how pioneers had built cabins that way hundreds of years ago. I decided that I would place two flat rocks under each girder along with a short post that would sit between the rock and beam, to support the girder if all else should fail. I would pound a re-bar pin through the girder and into the short post so the short post couldn't wiggle out. Assuming that frost heave didn't push up the post and tilt the girder, I thought it should work. So although I thought I didn't need the extra posts, I put them in anyway.

Sawmill & Roofing

For a long time I had thought about all the timber on our land and how nice it would be to have a band saw mill. We had so much timber on the property that the sawmill would eventually pay for itself, and we certainly had more time than we did money. I brought up the idea to my wife and explained the pros and cons about the sawmill. She thought it would be a good idea.

The problem was the initial cost. We had virtually no money to spend, and even *used* sawmills cost thousands of dollars if they can be found. It would take us all summer to save up that much money, and then we wouldn't have time to use it before winter came.

In late April we made the decision that instead of buying floor joists and plywood for the sub floor, we would save that money to buy a sawmill and cut our own joists and a solid wood 1" sub-floor. We had decided on the Harbor Freight sawmill. I had mixed feelings about Harbor Freight tools. Simple tools with few moving parts seemed to work well, while more complicated tools seemed to be hit or miss. And a sawmill was a complicated tool.

But I knew that Harbor Freight had a good return program if I was unhappy. I did a lot of reading online. People who owned the sawmill seemed to be happy with it, while the critics of the sawmill had never actually touched one. I am not a tool snob and I simply like what works.

I was excited to get the sawmill and start sawing boards but it would take us many weeks to save up the money.

On April 25th we picked up the roof panels and we had them temporarily installed within a couple hours. The retailer had made a mistake and given our roofing screws to another customer so I only had a few screws to work with that were left over from another project from years ago. By that time summer was coming in hot. My wife was back at the homestead and the daughter was staying with us on weekends until school would be out. All four of us worked on getting the roof panels up, with me on the roof and the other three unloading and handing up the 24 roof panels. The roof panels were each 3 feet wide and 16 feet long but not very heavy, and the only challenges were in keeping them from blowing out of control in the wind while they were being staged, and my struggle to drag them up to the roof without stepping through an opening and breaking my neck on my way down. I tacked each panel down with two screws. I waited for the rest of the screws to be returned to the retailers so we could pick them up and I could fasten down the panels completely.

As it turned out it took us a long time to get the missing screws but I didn't mind because the steel roof was more slippery than I thought it would be. I didn't look forward to walking around up there again. All summer long, every time the wind blew I thought about those missing roof screws and about how I needed to get them in before winter. I kept putting it off until finally it was October when I climbed back up there and spent a few hours with a rope tied around my waist and got the job done. I was relieved.

Installing the roofing

Spring 2014
Outdoor Kitchen

I OFTEN GET BORED working on the same thing over and over. After we got the roofing panels in place and as I was building the floor beams I did a lot of thinking about the cabin. I got the idea that I wanted to add an outdoor kitchen.

An outdoor kitchen can be an asset when living off grid. In an outdoor kitchen we can cook or bake with a wood stove or wood fired oven in the summer without bringing the extra heat into the house. And in the past I had always butchered chickens in the indoor kitchen sink. It's a messy job, and I would much prefer to do it outdoors, but unless I had a screened in area I would be pestered by bugs.

I wanted to place the outdoor kitchen on the north side of the house so that it would be cooler in summer. My plans included a counter top with a sink and drain, electrical receptacles and lights and space for a propane range, a wood cook stove and possibly a wood fired oven. We'd butcher chickens or small game in the sink, or process canned vegetables in the fall, or in a pinch, we could cook on the wood stove in the summer. The space would double as a deck where we could barbecue food and entertain friends, and I would enclose the sides with big screened windows to keep the bugs out.

I decided to make the floor of the outdoor kitchen about 15' x 15' because this lined up with the posts that were already in place and would it work with the lengths of old steel roofing I had lying around. This meant I had to install 5 more perimeter posts and a short post in the center to hold up the center floor beam.

So I spent some time digging more holes, felling more trees, peeling bark and charring post bottoms. Those posts were not as large as the cabin posts although they were still quite heavy. After I set them I had to install three rafters at the top, sloping gently down from the cabin eave purlin. Then I left the posts and went back to work cutting floor beams with the chain saw mill.

The outdoor kitchen area

Spring 2014
Bracing

I WAS CONCERNED about potential "racking" of the cabin. Racking is the tendency of the walls of the structure to lean. One way to prevent this is to add diagonal bracing between a vertical post and a horizontal beam or pole.

I had read that buried posts will counteract racking in something that is known as a cantilever effect. The post will resist leaning just by being buried in the ground. I also knew that plywood nailed to studs acts to prevent racking and in fact this is the bracing method used for most stick-built homes. I planned to install stud walls between each post and nail plywood on the exterior of the studs so I felt that any additional bracing I added was overkill. But I don't mind adding extra strength to anything I build, especially my house!

In late March I began adding some diagonal bracing. I wasn't sure how much I was going to add, but I wanted to at least get a feel for how much time it would take. It ended up taking quite awhile because I decided to first work on the gable ends and there were no horizontal beams on which to fasten the diagonal braces. My son and I set to work cutting and peeling 6-½' by 10" logs and hoisting them ten feet into the air to secure them in place as beams. To lift them into the air we used the pulley and the tractor.

We then had to cut and peel more logs, smaller this time at about 5" in diameter and about 4' long. Then I cut the ends at a perfect 45 degree angle and notched the posts and beams in exactly the right spot. After I set each brace in place I secured each end with at least one 6" spike.

I put most of the bracing on the gable ends. I decided that it took so much time to do that if I felt like I needed additional bracing in the long direction I would do it when I had available time and it probably wouldn't be until after we had moved in. In that case I would add the bracing at the tops of the interior posts where they meet the ridgepole and purlins. I had room to install twelve braces this way.

Most of my braces don't look pretty up close but they do the job. Later, I did not notice any racking at all but I still planned to add more bracing someday.

Spring 2014 Bracing

Corner Bracing

Horizontal poles on the gable end and diagonal bracing

Summer 2014
Sawmill

B Y THE SECOND OF JUNE we had saved up enough money to order the sawmill. The list price of the saw mill was $2499 but it had gone on sale for $1999. The only way to buy it was to call on the phone so my wife called Harbor Freight to order it. We had a 20% off coupon but we felt like they might not honor it on a big item that was on sale. In the end they did honor the coupon and my wife made the order. She can be persuasive.

Harbor Freight made some kind of error in the order and ended up taking off 25% instead of 20%. So the price of the sawmill was $1500 plus $100 for shipping. I picked up the sawmill at the shipping depot six days after I ordered it.

The sawmill is made of up two parts; the carriage and the track. The upper part is the carriage with four steel wheels at the bottom. At the top of the carriage is mounted a band saw assembly powered by a 7 horsepower gasoline engine. The engine powers the band saw blade which is 23 feet long long and about 1-1/4" wide. The carriage wheels roll on a nine foot long angle iron track. The whole thing is very heavy and weighs over 200 pounds.

A log is placed on the track and as the operator pushes the carriage down the length of the track, the saw cuts off the top of the log. The carriage is lowered with a hand crank mechanism and the process is repeated. Its very simple and it works very well.

I loved the sawmill and I spent the next couple months working on it every day, making floor joists and floor boards. After the

first week or two I ordered a set of ten blades from Cooks Blades
.

Over the summer I made about 800 square feet of 1" thick boards for the sub-floor and 600-700 linear feet of 2x5-½" floor joists. Sometimes my wife came out and enjoyed running the sawmill with me.

If you consider that lumber costs at least $2 per board foot, the floor boards alone paid for cost of the sawmill.

Summer 2014
Floor

O VER A PERIOD OF A COUPLE WEEKS my wife and kids helped me install all the floor joists. I toenailed them to the beams and the band joists. It was then that I learned how hard tamarack wood can be and I bent many nails.

I spent some time planning where the drain pipes would be placed under the floor, and on one of my wife's many trips to the city she bought the PVC fittings we would need. I followed all plumbing codes and allowed for vents near every future fixture. I planned it so almost all the drain lines would be consolidated into one pipe run that went parallel to and in between the joists so that I wouldn't have to drill through them. My only concern was how to prevent the shower trap from freezing so I built a box around it that would hold extra insulation. I found out later that it wasn't enough and the trap froze anyway.

I thought for some time about how I was going to insulate the floor. My first plan was to nail some 1x2s to the underside of the joists (and perpendicular to them) every couple feet to act as supports. Then from the top, we would drop in rigid styrofoam insulation so that it rested between the joists and on top of the 1x2s. Then on top of the rigid styrofoam we would add more insulation in the form of fiberglass or blow-in cellulose.

As it turned out we didn't have the money for the rigid styrofoam. The plan changed. I crawled beneath the joists and attached tar paper to the underside of the joists. Then we could fill the joist cavities with the blow-in cellulose insulation.

It took me a few days to attach the tar paper and it was a frustrating experience. There was only a couple vertical feet of room and I was hot and sweaty and constantly getting poked in the back with pine cones as I scooted along hammering plastic-capped nails to every joist.

I had some temporary boards on top of the joists for me to walk around topside. Two or three times the dogs would climb around up there on the boards and step off and wreck the tar paper so I had to go back and repair it. I might have fallen through a couple times myself also. I did some cussing over those couple days until we got the sub floor completely installed.

After I fastened the tar paper underneath, we bought the blow-in insulation from Lowes and got a free rental on the blower that is needed to install it. While my wife operated the blower and kept it full of cellulose, I operated the business end of the hose and filled in between all the joists. It was a very dusty and hot job.

By August 26th we had finished cutting all 110 floor joists and three quarters of the 1' thick floor boards. Most of the floor boards were 4" wide but we had cut many of them at 5" or 6" and some were seven or eight inches wide. I had been stacking the boards on sticks so that they could dry in the shade.

They were rough cut, direct from the sawmill so before we could install them on the floor we had to run them through the Dewalt planer to get them to a uniform thickness and have at least one smooth side. We had tried to cut them at just over 1" thick so that we could plane them down to 1". Most of them came out pretty close, but we had to do quite a lot of planing.

After planing we ran the boards through a table saw to make the edges as straight as possible and to provide a uniform width. I had to add an extra long sacrificial fence (made out of a straight 2x4) to the table saw to do this.

By August 27th I was ready to take a break from running the sawmill for awhile so I began fastening floorboards to the joists.

I used 3" long deck screws. My wife had scored a good deal on them at the home re-use store in Missoula where they sell left over building supplies for charity. She had installed a lot of the floor boards herself. It took awhile because many of the boards had somewhat of a crook to them even after running them through the table saw. We had to use a pipe clamp to straighten them out before we screwed them in so that the cracks between boards would be as small as possible.

By September 11th, we had finished installing all the floorboards and I was once again excited. It seemed we had reached another milestone!

Floor girders made with the chainsaw mill

First floor boards installed!

Angus approves of the new floor

FALL 2014
WALLS

ALTHOUGH THE DAYS WERE STILL VERY WARM, it was then nearly fall and the temperature was dipping into the twenties at night. We were motivated to get moved into the house before winter. It had been almost a year since we began work on the cabin but we were starting to see the light at the end of the tunnel.

Some time late in the summer my old beater pickup truck had broken a piston. I was upset that we no longer had a four wheel drive vehicle and we didn't have any way to transport big materials. My wife's dad felt bad for us and gave us his old cargo van which was a good thing because we didn't have money to buy something else. It wasn't four wheel drive but it would do until we got big snow so we were thankful.

I immediately began working on building the exterior stud walls. We had only one generator at the time; Big Red, and every day I had to roll it from the camper to the cabin, a distance of a couple hundred feet over rough terrain. At the end of the day I rolled it back to the camper. It was exhausting to do, or maybe I was getting worn out from the constant work.

All the stud walls were built from re-claimed 2x4s that my wife bought at a really good price from the home re-use store. The studs had once been in the walls of old buildings that had been demolished and it felt kind of strange to know that our new walls might be a hundred years old. We wondered about their history.

My wife also scored an excellent deal on some reclaimed ½" plywood for about three dollars a sheet. I had to pull out a few nails and work around some odd holes but we used it for almost all the exterior sheathing. She also bought eight big windows for $10 each and many other things we used during our construction.

While we were working on the exterior walls I kept wondering where we were going to get a water tank. We had been searching craigslist for weeks hoping to find a good deal on one and in late September we finally found it. A man had a 275 gallon IBC tote for $150. The tote was food grade and he had used it to supply water for his horses.

We called the seller and found out that he was willing to trade the tank for a truckload of firewood. I didn't have any way to pick it up (it wouldn't fit in the van) but he was willing to drive over with it to the cabin and make the trade. He was a really nice low keyed retired guy. He didn't mind the drive and mostly did it for the scenery. My impression was that he didn't need the money too bad and could afford to buy firewood but simply liked to trade for stuff. It was an enjoyable experience.

My cost was one day's work of dragging various downed trees to a spot and cutting them into four foot sections and helping to load them into the truck. It decreased my supply of easy-to-get firewood but we were very happy with the trade.

The tank wouldn't fit through the door but I used the come-along again and moved it into the cabin through a window opening. I later set it up in the loft area over the bathroom. I had installed 4x8 tamarack beams there spaced every two feet and I had looked up the load calculations. They could easily support the one ton of water that the tank would hold.

At the beginning of October we had finished all the exterior wall studs and sheathing.

I had been wondering for some time how we were going to heat the new cabin. The plan was to find a used stove on craigslist but like usual, we didn't have the money. Things always work out in the end. During one of our visits to our neighbors who lived down the easement road, we talked about our search for a wood stove. They mentioned that they had an old stove in their garage and that we could have it if we wanted it. Of course we accepted and were very grateful.

I built a temporary hearth out of some fiber cement board and some rock wool. We had a few inside stud walls by then (but only studs, no drywall or anything) and I didn't want the studs behind the stove to catch fire. I built a heat shield for the wall with some left over roofing, spacing it from the wall about an inch with some small pieces of copper pipe.

The stove was a very heavy Hearthstone model with a soapstone lined, two cubic foot fire box. My son and I drove the old cargo van to the neighbors' garage and loaded it up by using some scrap 2x4s as ramps and hooking the come-along into the van and winching the stove up the ramps.

We moved the stove into the cabin again using the come-along to get the stove out of the van and up onto the porch, and we put the stove on the hearth. I had recently fastened down the steel roof panels with what seemed like a million roofing screws trying to beat the winter, but I had to go up on the roof again to work on the new chimney. It was a cold rainy day on that slippery roof while I installed the flashing and the triple wall chimney pipe. Once again I was glad when it was over.

I installed the stovepipe and ceiling adapter that we had used at the camper. I had to modify it somewhat but it fit perfectly and kept the required distance between the chimney pipe and any combustible materials.

I started a fire in the stove that night just because I could. As I sat in an old lawn chair I watched the flames and thought about the work that I had yet to do.

By October 20th we had finished covering the exterior of the cabin with house wrap. The windows and the two exterior doors were not installed and for the next few days we worked on installing the doors. We had bought them both at the home re-use store for about $90 total. They were nice steel shelled doors that just needed a little paint. One was pre-hung and was easy enough to install. The other was a simple door slab and we needed to build a jamb. I was busy working on something or other so my wife looked up on the internet how to build a door jamb. She then looked through the scrap wood and, finding a few pieces she liked she set about cutting them on the table saw and planing them to the right thickness. I helped her assemble the door to the jamb and I mounted it the next morning.

On October 25th we officially moved into the cabin. With the old van we had brought some of our furniture out of storage and it was good to sleep in a real bed again. But more than that it felt good to finally be in our new home. There was no insulation in the walls or ceiling yet and no kitchen or toilet but we had finally moved in.

Five days later we began installing the insulation in the ceiling. It was fiberglass insulation meant for 2x4 walls. That way I would have a gap at the top to allow passive ventilation in the hopes of preventing condensation. It took a few days and a lot of work on ladders.

In November we put fiberglass insulation in the exterior walls. I had to cut a lot of triangles to fit the areas where I had put the diagonal bracing but other than that it was a boring, tedious process that made a lot of dust. As usual I was glad to be done with it.

We also worked on making a temporary kitchen counter and some shelves out of scrap wood so that we would have a way to cook food and store some of our many pots and pans and dishes. My wife spent some time making kitchen counters out of leftover scrap wood; picking out wood scraps, cutting them on the table saw and planing them, then gluing them together and sanding and finishing. The counters look unbelievably good and it seemed that my wife was turning into a very handy woodworker!

She had bought an enameled cast iron sink and a faucet at the home re-use store and I set it into the cutout I had made in the counter. I put some buckets underneath to catch the drain water. We brought in jugs of water to cook with and to wash dishes, and we showered at the camper.

I built a temporary shelf to hold the Coleman stove until we could afford to buy a used propane range. It worked very well but we still had no oven. Sometimes we cooked things by using the dutch oven set on the wood stove. We managed to cook pizza by setting it on a clay pizza plate and covering it with a big cast iron frying pan.

By that time I had moved the solar panels and batteries from the camper and I had run some temporary electrical lines to some receptacles and lighting fixtures. We weren't getting a lot of solar power at that time of year so we ran the generator often. I had installed the digital TV and the satellite dish as well. As I said to my daughter, "We may not have running water yet but by God we can watch The Walking Dead in glorious 1080p resolution!"

I had decided that I wanted to try to use 12 Volt DC LED lighting. I found a supplier from China on ebay who was selling 5 Watt bulbs 12 Volt bulbs with an E26/E27 base so they will screw into a regular residential light socket. I ordered ten and put them into some of the fixtures my wife had bought used at the home re-use store and wired it to a 12 Volt DC fuse panel. It is not the brightest light in the world but it uses very little power and will work if the inverter breaks.

Exterior walls almost complete

House wrap is on and the chimney is installed

The water tank

Fall 2014
Greywater Part II

O   N November 5th I finally got around to finishing the grey water system so that we could have a sink without buckets underneath the drains. I had been working on it for the past month because it required a lot of hand digging.

My thinking was that all drain waste water from the cabin would drain into a pit filled with straw bales. We would also have a flush toilet and that will drain into the pit. The toilet would be for peeing only; other stuff would have to be done at the composting toilet until we could get a real septic system installed. I wanted a safe, clean way to discharge household water. Urine is okay to mix with straw because it is rich in nitrogen and will react with the carbon in the straw to make compost. We probably wouldn't use the compost to grow edible plants but the option was there. One important part of the plan was that I wanted the pit to be freeze-proof, which is why I made it so deep.

First I dug a 28 foot long trench leading to a 3'x4' pit, 3-½' deep. I dug it by hand with a shovel and pick-ax which is why it took so long. I hoped that if the pit is deep and filled with straw and there is composting action down below, the contents at the bottom should not ever freeze.

Then I started laying 3" pipe and filled the pit with straw bales. It took 6 straw bales total. I used straw bales because I wanted a deep, freeze-proof, method, and I had some old moldy straw bales lying around. I also had a lot of wood chips lying around and was thinking about using them but it was easier to throw the bales in there and I felt like they would make good insulation.

Then I cut the bottoms off two plastic planter pots and cut a hole in one for the pipe. I stacked them together for the pipe to run into and to make an access point. I placed a bucket lid over the access point.

With the access hole I could check on how things are going when, for example, we did a load of laundry. If I didn't get enough drainage I could punch some holes in the planter pots or figure something else out. There was at least a foot of straw underneath the drainage hole and it worked according to plan in the freezing weather.

I had done some research on the depth of the drain pipe. Most codes say it needs to be deep but a lot of plumbers seem to feel that the waste water temperature is above freezing and in any case its not in the pipe long enough to freeze. In fact many older houses in cold areas have shallow pipes and as long as they get no blockages they work fine. So I did not worry about putting the drain pipe below frost depth and it did not freeze.

We got some plumbing parts to install the trap under the kitchen sink and we then had a real sink drain. We didn't have running water yet so I cobbled together a way to run water from the IBC tote to the RV pump I had stolen from the camper. I then ran some PEX pipe from there to the sink and I celebrated.

Then I installed the toilet my wife had brought home from the home re-use store. Then the girls celebrated because they were tired of peeing in the woods!

I did some more plumbing work and ran some more PEX pipe. We fetched the washing machine from the camper and after the ice in it had thawed we could wash clothes in the cabin. We hung a line by the stove and hung the wet clothes there to dry them.

We still didn't have hot water so I robbed the camper of its little electric water heater and ran some more PEX lines and we had hot water to the sink. The only thing missing was a shower. My wife wanted to build a nice tiled shower but we would have to save up for it. And I still wasn't sure if I was happy with my insulated shower trap plan.

In the mean time I had to do something so we could shower at home instead of at the neighbors' house. I hated to intrude on them like that but the water in the camper was now frozen. So I came up with a crude idea that worked. Like a lot of things in the cabin it was temporary but it did the job.

I had a good sized rubber livestock water tank that held 50 gallons or so. With a hole saw I made a hole in the bottom of the tank the size of the shower drain. I assembled the drain fitting onto the tank. I then set the tank and drain on the floor so that the drain fitting went over the shower drain pipe that poked up through the floor.

Then I ran some more PEX pipe to an old shower faucet my wife had found at the home re-use store and I installed the shower head with a quarter turn stop valve in line just before it. Those plumbing parts were all installed directly onto the the studs as we did not yet have any sheet rock installed.

At the ceiling, I suspended a hoop made out of a piece of PEX pipe to serve as a circular shower curtain rod. I hung two shower curtains on it so that they overlapped. They dropped down into the basin.

I tested it out the new shower and it worked great. We had hot showers in the cabin!

Excavating for the grey water system

Pipe added to the trench

Filling the pit with straw bales

Complete except for burying the pipe

Access hole

Winter 2014
Moved In

A T THE TIME OF THIS WRITING it is January 2015 and we are spending our first winter in the cabin. For Christmas, my wife cooked a large dinner to prove that it can be done with our simple kitchen. She cooked the turkey in the big pressure canner on the Coleman stove and it was quite delicious.

We still have a lot of work to do. There are no real interior walls so there isn't much privacy (we have sheets hung on the studs around the bathroom) and there are four windows left to be installed. The window holes are filled with insulation.

But we have a sink with running water, a hot shower, a wood stove and warm beds to sleep in at night. I suppose we can go on indefinitely this way if we need to and it's just in time. We spent any extra money we had on Christmas presents for the kids and now we're hoping to get a slightly less unreliable four wheel drive vehicle so that I can stop pulling the car up the icy hill with the tractor.

My wife, daughter and son are living here and they tough it out without complaint.

It feels good to live here and I have no regrets.

The new wood stove

Temporary Kitchen

Part Four
To Survive and Thrive

CAN WE TRULY LIVE A SUSTAINABLE LIFE?

I AM AT THE BEGINNING of my homestead journey. I still have plenty of work to do to get to where I want to be. I don't know if we will get to building our dream log cabin but perhaps someday we might. Within the next few years I want to be able to grow most of my own food for my family and my livestock and build a root cellar to store it in. I want to produce most of our energy; we plan to expand the solar power system (I discuss my solar power system in the section on "Power") by adding more panels and we are thinking about adding a small wind turbine. In the summer I want to build a solar hot water system and by next winter I want to be able to heat all our cold-season hot water with the wood stove. I plan to start a permaculture food forest and to fence in more acreage for some pigs. I want to finish the outdoor kitchen. A homesteader's work seems to be endless but it's the kind of work that I like doing.

But will I ever get to the point where I will be living a sustainable life?

The short answer is not without making major changes to my lifestyle. For example, I like salt. I have no way to produce salt. So if I want to live a sustainable life I will need to figure out how to not use salt. It is true that I can stockpile great quantities of salt for relatively little money (and that is what I do) but that is not "sustainable".

I can't produce cane sugar but I can theoretically produce honey or grow sweet sorghum or sugar beets. I'd like to try to grow them all some day.

Other things may be possible to produce. If I wanted to make my own beer I would need barley, some kind of sugar, and hops. It is possible that I can produce or grow those things. But what about yeast?

Still, a lot of things that I do on the homestead are centered around the goal of being able to live without outside inputs. But in the mean time I will use what I can and later if I need to, I will adjust. My ultimate goal is to *survive*. I'm talking about surviving without food from the grocery store or fuel for my generator, tractor, or chainsaw.

To survive we need food, water and shelter.

Food

Food and water are the most important elements to survival. They can be stockpiled, but I'm not wanting to simply live from stores of food (it will eventually run out) and I'm also not talking about foraging for wild food. There are edible wild plants and some people can forage to survive in the woods but there are two problems with that idea. First I don't have the skills. Second, I don't feel that it is possible in any but the most perfect conditions. Looking out my window I see evergreen trees and six inches of snow on the ground. I could make some pine-needle tea and scrape up a few rose hips but how could I find enough calories to support myself and my family? I could take a few squirrels with the .22 rifle, but how many squirrels are there and what do I do when my ammunition runs out? Or when the neighbors are shooting the same squirrels and they have all disappeared?

Organic Gardening

I want to be able to *produce* food indefinitely and this means gardening. And doing it without inputs such as petroleum based fertilizers, herbicides and pesticides. And without using equipment that requires parts or fuel, like a tractor. I'm not against using powered equipment; I simply want to have a means to grow food *without it* if I need to.

Gardening without chemical additives means *organic gardening*. To garden in a sustainable way we need to grow food organically.

In my opinion organic gardening is healthier. When I first read about Monsanto corn I learned that the corn is genetically modified to be able to withstand being sprayed with Round-Up. All the weeds around the corn will die from the poison, but the corn will thrive. Aside from the potential problems with genetic engineering, why would I want to eat food that has been sprayed with Round-Up? I heard an interview with Michael Pollan where he told a story about potato farmers in Idaho. Because the potato plants had been sprayed with powerful pesticides, the potatoes had to be stored, isolated for six months after harvest to off-gas the poisons. The farmers themselves grew little patches of organic potatoes at home for their own consumption.

But the biggest reason to grow organically is because if we are concerned with being somewhat self-sustainable we won't have access to chemicals and we must provide our own fertilizer. The most common way to provide that is in the form of animal manure. Chickens, rabbits, goats, and cows provide excellent fertilizer. There is more physical labor involved in the form of moving the manure to the growing fields, unless we can have the animals deposit the fertilizer where it is needed. One way to do this is to have two rotating growing fields and have the animals fenced in the field not being used. Chickens and pigs are excellent for this purpose. Chickens will eat insects and weed seedlings and pigs will root up the ground looking for grubs and roots. When combined, they can do a lot of the work in preparing a field for the next year's planting.

Controlling insect pests organically can be more difficult. The chickens will eat some of the ground-bearing pests before planting but there will be other pests. I have heard that Guinea fowl will walk through a garden and eat the bugs off plants without harming the crops (unlike chickens who will gleefully eat the tomatoes). Ducks love to eat slugs (of course so do chickens!) but it may be best to find out what varieties of plants are the most pest resistant in the local area. This is where years of practice at gardening really pays off, and why we need to start now and not wait until it is too late.

There have been hundreds of books written on organic gardening and I won't pretend to be such an expert at it that I can write a chapter about it. I have a few books on the subject by Rodale Press and I recommend that every homesteader start reading those.

I think learning to garden should start with learning the soil. In my opinion the best book about this subject is *The Gardener's Guide to Better Soil*, by Gene Logsdon. The book is old and out of print but it really opened my eyes about how important soil is and what we can do to improve it.

What Foods Do We Need?

If we are making a point about what food to grow to survive we should spend most of our time not thinking so much about calories, but about *protein*.

It is relatively easy to find food in the wild - dandelions and stinging nettle and so forth. But we need a lot of protein to survive so it should be our main focus. When we think about typical garden crops; tomatoes, cabbage, potatoes, and carrots, there is just not much protein there. It is true that a person could practically live on potatoes, but he would have to eat 5-10 pounds every day! Can you say "food fatigue?"

We need to have sources of protein that are easy to grow and harvest. For this reason every survival homestead should prioritize beans and livestock, and by livestock I'm talking about chickens or ducks. (The birds can be eaten after they get a few years old but they will produce eggs in the mean time.)

Like Henry David Thoreau, beans are highest on my list of protein plants. Thoreau planted miles of rows of beans next to his cabin in the woods. Aside from being a good source of protein they are fairly easy to grow, easy to reproduce from seed, and can be dried to last for years. In addition, beans are nitrogen fixers, meaning they will pull nitrogen from the air and add it to the soil when you till in the plants after harvest!

Gardening author Carol Deppe seems to agree with the "beans and eggs" idea. In her book *The Resilient Gardener: Food Production and Self-Reliance in Uncertain Times* she focuses on beans, potatoes, corn and squash, with a small flock of chickens or ducks to supply eggs. These five foods will give us almost everything we need to live on and are easier to harvest than wheat or other grains. In addition, those garden crops can be stored all winter long in a root cellar, something to think about if we may be gardening in an isolated location without the benefit of modern conveniences. Although Ms Deppe's climate is the coastal northwest, she explains in great detail why she chose those basic five foods and how she grows them.

Steve Solomon emphasizes similar ideas and relates good experience in growing food to survive in a drier climate in his book *Gardening When It Counts: Growing Food in Hard Times*. Steve works primitively, double digging his garden with a shovel, and he gardens the old fashioned way with a lot of space between plants so they have room to reach water and minerals. This is how it was done in the 19th century and it seems to be a practical way to do it if we have the room.

Dairy is another good source of protein. A small goat can provide milk and with milk we can make cheese which can be stored in a root cellar. But milking is a big commitment, usually needing to be performed twice a day in a clean facility and the milk must be stored somewhere. I learned the hard way that this commitment should be taken only after most of the homestead is established. My two goats are four years old and I haven't yet started milking them.

I am by no means a vegetarian and I love to eat meat! Common homestead sources of meat are cattle, goats, chickens (or other birds), pigs, and rabbits, and meat brought to the table in the form of hunting wild game.

I would like to raise some miniature cattle in the future. The meat-to-feed ratio is supposedly better than with a full sized breed and the mini cows need less grazing space. If intensive rotational grazing techniques are used (as advocated by Joel Salatin) even less space may be required.

I've never tried goat meat and our goats are more pets than livestock, but if times were desperate I would eat them, assuming they weren't able to produce milk.

I hate to think of confining any livestock animal. As I said, I love to eat meat but I prefer that the animal was raised healthy and happily. Pasture raised or free ranged livestock meets those requirements. For example, pigs don't have to come with a bad smell but when they are confined to a small pen, the pen will stink. Pigs have other benefits besides bacon! They can prepare an area for planting by rooting the ground in search of grubs and roots and prepare an area for a pond or they can be set loose in a briar patch and clear it out.

Many homesteaders breed rabbits for protein. I don't have a lot of experience in this area, although we did have rabbit pets for a few years and they were easy to care for. I have heard about diseases affecting rabbits but it seems to me that if you can get a healthy den going and isolate them from other rabbits they would stay healthy.

As for other plant foods, corn is a good source of sugars and carbohydrates. But takes a lot of space and is a nitrogen hog, meaning it will deplete the soil of that valuable element. However, I love corn so I grow it. I have planted a variety called Painted Mountain Corn, which I purchased from http://rockymountaincorn.com. This is not sweet corn, but is an open pollinated field corn bred specifically to survive in the Rocky Mountains in poor soil. The price for a pound of seed at the time of this writing is about $30, but seed can be saved from the crop for next year's planting.

Fruit will provide vitamin C and nuts can provide protein and oils. Trees should be planted as soon as possible to allow them time to establish and start producing. I'm not fond of dwarf fruit trees - they are vulnerable to damage by deer, especially if left alone at an isolated location and in my experience they don't seem to be as hearty as the full size varieties. But if they can be contained in tall deer-proof fencing, dwarf trees can be an option and sometimes they do start producing earlier.

I've planted a few blackberry bushes on the property. They have a reputation for getting out of control but my thinking is that it would be a good thing. If I become overrun with food producing plants I'll decide that things could be worse.

In my area I've had good luck with raspberries and strawberries. When planting strawberries I like to put them in the ground with a mix of half composted manure and half soil. If watered well they will produce like crazy and can be preserved in the form of strawberry jam.

Cash crops should always be given consideration. My soil is slightly acidic and I would like to plant blueberries which might bring a substantial income at a farmer's market. But what other items will sell? The general strategy is to visit the local farmer's market and observe what sells for the most money. Combine this with produce that will be valuable to ourselves. For example, in many farmer's markets the thing that sells the most is cut flowers! But that won't help you survive, so what about exotic berries? I've been thinking about Seaberry, also known as Sea Buckthorn. It is a tall shrub from Asia which produces nutritious and medicinal berries and can survive in a cold harsh environment. In addition, Seaberry is a nitrogen fixer, meaning it will pull nitrogen from the air and add it to the soil in the form of dropped leaves and twigs. So it is a natural fertilizer and can serve three purposes: an income opportunity, a source of food and vitamin C, and it improves the soil around it.

How Much Land?

THIS IS A QUESTION on the mind of every potential homesteader. How much land do we need to be able to grow enough food for ourselves? What about a woodlot, space for buildings and roads, and room for livestock? Variables include climate, soil condition, skills of the gardener, exposure to the sun, and rainfall.

There are stories of people feeding themselves on a quarter of an acre using intensive gardening techniques and imported fertilizer. Others say we need a hundred acres. Due to environmental variables and different levels of farming skills there is no definite answer but my opinion is that more land is better.

In the table below I have summarized some commercial crop production yields for the year of 2012 in the state of Montana . I edited the data by cutting the production yields in half for two reasons: to be conservative and to adjust for farming with small scale organic techniques rather than large scale, industrial type farming with added chemical fertilizers and pesticides. In addition I have added a column to show calories produced per acre and a column to show how many days worth of food this would produce, based on a daily caloric intake of 2,700 calories. I admit the last column is somewhat arbitrary and is there only to show a frame of reference. It's hard to read a number like 7,191,000 calories and deduce any meaning; thus the extra column.

Food	Homesteading Pounds per Acre	Calories per Acre	2,700 Calorie Days
Sugar beets	28200	7,191,000	2663
Dry beans	750	1,182,955	438
Dry edible peas	750	143,182	53
Lentils	550	882,500	327
Wheat	1047	1,565,741	580
Barley	1272	2,046,764	758
Oats	720	1,273,091	472
Corn for grain	3080	4,774,000	1768
Potatoes	750	261,750	97
Totals		**19,320,982**	**7156**

From the table we can see that if we planted 10 acres of sugar beets, dry beans, and the rest of the foods from above, and assuming we had good production of all crops, we would have enough food for one person to last 7,156 days. Or enough food to feed 19 people for one year:

$$7{,}156 \text{ calorie days} \div 365 \text{ days} = 19$$

From this we can calculate that if we plant one tenth of an acre with each of the foods above (for a total of one acre of land) we could almost feed two people (1.9) for a year.

So in theory two people could grow enough food to survive with a garden sized at just over one acre. But how will we fertilize the garden? Maybe there should be an additional acre set aside so that crops can be rotated and a cover crop such as rye, clover or vetch may be grown in the non-producing field. Perhaps an acre should be set aside for free ranging chickens, so that chicken manure can be collected from the coop and used for fertilizer. Another option is to run the chickens in the fallow field and they will eat pests and fertilize without our help, and the next year the chickens can be rotated to the other field and so on. Based on this logic, a minimum of three acres would be required to grow food for two people.

In the section later on Livestock Feed it is stated that an acre should be set aside to grow chicken feed for ten chickens. We are now up to three or four acres. If we need to support other livestock we will need additional space.

I would set aside at least half an acre for buildings and driveways.

I would also set aside some land for fruit and nut trees and berry bushes. These can take up a lot of space. But fruit trees and berry shrubs can be planted around the house or along the driveways as edible (and stealthy) landscaping plants, or planted along the south edge of the garden. With a little creative thinking we can get a lot of plants in a limited space. I will never plant a purely ornamental shrub, it should have some value as food or some other benefit.

There are other perennial foods that should be considered. Jerusalem Artichoke (sometimes called "sun chokes") can be planted along fence lines. Asparagus can be planted in part shade and will produce for 25 years or more, and rhubarb can be planted in shady little areas by the porch.

An herb garden can be planted near the house for easy access from the kitchen. If left to go to seed it may regrow the following year.

A woodlot is important and should be considered a source of not only firewood but also of building materials. I use timber from my property whenever I can for everything from the structure of my cabin and the chicken coop to the shelves in the pantry. The required size of the woodlot will be determine by the species of trees and how fast they grow, how dense the timber is (in terms of BTUs per pound when considering firewood) and the climate.

I would like to set aside an acre or so to grow Black Locust trees which add nitrogen to the soil, provide food for bees and birds (there are good reasons to keep birds around; they eat pest insects for one thing), and they grow very fast and can be coppiced, meaning they can be chopped down and re-grow from the stump. In addition, the wood is very dense, makes good tool handles and firewood and is rot resistant. There are tales of Black Locust fence posts that re-sprout after being set in the ground!

The size of the woodlot will vary as stated, but considering a cold winter climate and potential building materials I might not be happy with anything less than 2-3 acres dedicated to that purpose. The running land total is now up to at least six and a half acres, and I think we can safely say that is the bare minimum that should be considered.

Having said that, I feel it would be better to pay outright for three acres than take out a 30-year mortgage on twenty acres. Having three acres paid for may be a benefit that outweighs the productivity of more land. And it may not be possible to find the right amount of land with the present budget, or perhaps a large amount of acreage simply can't be found. The point I'm making is to get the most land you can afford and start working from there.

Permaculture

Some time ago I was introduced to the concept of permaculture. The premise is that instead of separating production of annual food crops by species, perennial plants are grown together in a way in which the plants provide benefits to the plants around them. A group of these symbiotic plants is called a "guild". The plants in the guild feed us and feed each other and the soil, all with minimal input from us. This mimics nature, but is directed toward producing an output that benefits us. Some of the plants add nitrogen to the soil, some repel insects, some attract beneficial insects, some provide food, and some do all the above.

A typical permaculture guild might have an apple tree planted at its center. Around the perimeter will be chives to repel pest insects, daffodils and dill to attract pollinators, and toward the base of the tree will be planted comfrey to add nitrogen to the soil. You could add strawberry or bearberry plants to act as a ground cover.

All the plants in the guild are edible or medicinal, and all have a second purpose; to benefit the guild.

An offshoot to the concept of permaculture is the Food Forest. The idea is to plant a bunch of guilds in close proximity and create a self-sustaining forest of food producing perennials. With very little input the food forest will keep producing for decades. Another benefit to the food forest is that it is a "stealth" garden. A stranger might walk right through the middle of a food forest and not realize it. In terms of a stealthy homestead this can be a serious advantage.

I have not yet started my permaculture garden so I don't have first hand experience with it. Permaculture is a a huge topic so having introduced it, I will suggest further reading. There are dozens of books on the subject of permaculture and I have a bunch of them. For beginners I would recommend *Gaia's Garden*, by Toby Hemenway, and *The Vegetable Gardener's Guide to Permaculture: Creating an Edible Ecosystem*, by Christopher Shein. For an excellent reference guide to plant relationships and theory on food forests I recommend *Edible Forest Gardens, Volume II*, by Dave Jacke and Eric Toensmeier.

Livestock Feed

I have a symbiotic relationship with my livestock. They provide food and fertilizer for me but I need to be able to feed and water them. In the summer my chickens and goats could survive without additional feed but in the winter when the ground is beneath four feet of snow, the chickens will not be able to find food. So I keep in mind that I need to grow winter food for them. I would like to get a few miniature cattle and maybe some pigs. I'll need to be able to feed them as well.

In my opinion, no homestead should be without chickens. They provide meat and eggs, help control the bug population, they can forage on their own for most of the year, they're disease resistant, require very little maintenance and can reproduce on their own. In addition, their waste is considered some of the best organic fertilizer available. But during the winter months in Montana, chickens need to be fed. Currently we pick up bags of feed at the local feed store. But what if I want to grow food for them?

Harvey Ussery has a great book on raising chickens called *The Small-Scale Poultry Flock*. In it he has five chapters dedicated to chicken feed. I recommend this book for anyone serious about learning how to feed chickens directly from the homestead.

To summarize, Harvey recommends a small amount of natural minerals and vitamins such as kelp and fish meal making up 15% of the feed. I will assume those might be unavailable in our self-sustaining lifestyle (or will be found in another way), and the birds will have to get most of their vitamins and minerals by foraging in the summer. The bulk of the rest of the feed, and the parts we are mostly concerned with here, are made up of corn, peas, wheat, and oats.

Adjusting Harvey's percentages to subtract the vitamins and minerals, our chicken feed will consist of:

32% corn

23% peas

33% wheat

12% oats

* Any vitamins and minerals I could provide would be a bonus.

In order to keep things simple for the calculations later in this section, I will consider chicken feed in sacks of 100 pounds. So we'll estimate that a 100lb sack of home-grown chicken feed has 32lbs corn, 23lbs peas, 33lbs wheat, and 12lbs oats.

A chicken needs about 1.5 pounds of feed per week. If we assume a flock of ten chickens, that's 15 pounds of feed per week. Assuming that our ten chickens can forage during the summer and we need to feed our bird

15lbs x 24 weeks = 360lbs.

And:

$360\text{lbs} \div 100\text{lbs}/\text{sack} = 3.6$ sacks

To create the following table I used the same data source I used to create the table on homesteader food production. The table will help us calculate how much land we need to grow food for our ten chickens.

One 100lb Sack of Chicken Feed	Amount per Feed Sack (lbs)	Yield Per Acre (lbs)	Yield Per Sq Ft (lbs)	Space Required to Grow One Feed Sack (acres)	Space Required to Grow One Feed Sack (sq feet)	Yield if One Total Acre Planted (lbs)
Corn	32	3,080	0.07	0.01	453	986
Peas	23	750	0.02	0.03	1,336	173
Wheat	33	1,047	0.02	0.03	1,373	346
Oats	12	720	0.02	0.02	726	86
Totals	100			0.09	3,887	1,590

The first two columns in the above table are the ingredients needed to make up one 100lb sack of chicken feed.

Columns three and four, "Yield Per Acre" and "Yield Per Sq Ft" identify how much an acre or square foot would provide if planted entirely with the ingredient in each row. Their only purpose here is to help us provide calculations.

Columns five and six, "Space Required to Grow One Feed Sack", identify the space required of each ingredient to grow a complete 100lb feed sack, based on the data in the previous columns.

The last column is how many pounds of each ingredient would be provided if one acre was planted with 32% corn, 23% peas, 33% wheat, and 12% oats.

(The numbers are taken from an Excel spreadsheet and are rounded. If the math is double checked with these rounded numbers, *slightly* different results will be obtained.)

As stated earlier, a chicken needs about 1.5 pounds of feed per week. In order to find how much land we need to grow 360 pounds of feed (or 3.6 sacks), we need to do some math.

According to the table, we can see that we can grow 100 pounds of chicken feed on 0.09 acres, or 3,887 square feet, which is a plot of land about 63 feet by 63 feet. (There are 43,560 square feet in an acre).

If we want to provide 360 pounds of feed, we need to multiply the amount of land by 3.6, because we need 3.6 sacks of feed:

$$360lbs \div 100lbs = 3.6$$

and

$$3.6 \times .09 \text{ acres} = 0.324 \text{ acres}$$

A plot of land sized at 0.324 acres equals 14,113 square feet, or a square approximately 118' x 118'.

According to the table, if we dedicate an entire acre to growing chicken feed, we can produce 1,590 pounds of feed That's enough to feed 44 chickens for 24 weeks:

$$1,590lbs \text{ per acre} \div 1.5lbs \text{ per chicken} = 1,060 \text{ chicken/weeks}$$

and

$$1,060 \text{ chicken/weeks} \div 24 \text{ weeks} = 44 \text{ chickens}$$

The table on the following page is a chart detailing the amount of feed (in pounds) and acreage required to feed 10-100 chickens for five different lengths of time, from 10 weeks to a full year.

Weeks to Feed & Acres Required									
Qty of Chickens	10 Weeks	Req. Acres	20 Weeks	Req. Acres	30 Weeks	Req. Acres	40 Weeks	Req. Acres	52 Weeks	Req. Acres
10	150	0.09	300	0.19	450	0.28	600	0.38	780	0.49
20	300	0.19	600	0.38	900	0.57	1,200	0.75	1,560	0.98
30	450	0.28	900	0.57	1,350	0.85	1,800	1.13	2,340	1.47
40	600	0.38	1,200	0.75	1,800	1.13	2,400	1.51	3,120	1.96
50	750	0.47	1,500	0.94	2,250	1.42	3,000	1.89	3,900	2.45
60	900	0.57	1,800	1.13	2,700	1.70	3,600	2.26	4,680	2.94
70	1,050	0.66	2,100	1.32	3,150	1.98	4,200	2.64	5,460	3.43
80	1,200	0.75	2,400	1.51	3,600	2.26	4,800	3.02	6,240	3.92
90	1,350	0.85	2,700	1.70	4,050	2.55	5,400	3.40	7,020	4.42
100	1,500	0.94	3,000	1.89	4,500	2.83	6,000	3.77	7,800	4.91

To use the chart, find the number of chickens you want to feed in the first column. Then find the column with the number of weeks you want to feed them.

The number in the "Weeks" column is the amount of feed (in pounds) needed to feed the chickens for that number of weeks. The number to the right of each "Weeks" column is the acreage required to grow that amount of feed.

For example, if you wanted to feed 30 chickens for 40 weeks, find the row that has 30 chickens in the left-most column. Then follow the row over to the column which says "40 Weeks". That column has 1,800 pounds as the total feed required.

The number to the right of the "Weeks" column is 1.13. S0 to grow 1,800lbs of chicken feed to support 30 chickens for 40 weeks, you would need 1.62 acres.

WATER

ATER is the most important resource. In the planning of a homestead, water has the highest priority. If a property can be found which has a supply of surface water things are easier. However, properties with creeks, streams, or springs demand a premium price tag.

Wells

If no surface water is available the next best thing is a reliable well.

First, I'll explain how a well pump works in a typical grid-connected house. The system consists of the well pump, a pressure tank, and a pressure switch. The water is pumped from the well into the pressure tank. Inside the pressure tank is a waterproof bladder containing some air. As water enters the pressure tank it pushes against the bladder and this creates pressure in the tank.

The pressure switch has two positions: one turns on the well pump and the other turns it off. A typical pressure switch might be called a 40/60. This means it turns on the well pump if the pressure drops below 40 psi, and turns it off when enough water has entered the pressure tank to bring it up to 60 psi. The larger the pressure tank is, the more water it will hold before it trips the 60 psi position and turns off the pump. This ensures that the pump doesn't cycle on and off every time someone opens a faucet, saving wear and tear on the expensive well pump (it is healthier for the pump to run for a few long cycles than for many short cycles).

In a grid-connected house the pressure tank system works efficiently. But off-grid we may not have a constant 240V AC power to the well. In my case it only runs when the generator is hooked up to it and running. Even if we did have enough solar and batteries to supply a constant 240V, I would not want it cycling on and off all day, but only when I had enough power; when the sun is shining.

So the way it is typically done in an off-grid situation (where electrical energy is precious) is to use the generator to run the well pump and fill up a large storage tank. Those people with enough solar power capacity can fill the tank when the sun shines or use a small DC powered slow pump if the well is not too deep. Then we may have a second, small, DC powered pump (or in some cases an inverter-driven AC pump) to supply water to the fixtures.

If we have the proper terrain, we could keep the water storage tank uphill from the house or on a tower, negating the need for a second pump altogether. This tank would need to be very high relative to the house: water only exerts a pressure of 0.433 psi per vertical foot. Most of us are used to at least 40 psi at our fixtures so the tank would need to be elevated at least 92 feet high to develop that kind of pressure. But if the house is substantially downhill from the storage tank it can be done, and in a freezing climate the whole works could be buried to be kept from freezing.

Shallow wells are better than deep wells. Wells under 300 feet deep can be fitted with a hand pump or wind-driven pump. Bison hand pumps can be used to 300 feet. There is a company called Simple Pump which manufactures a hand-driven pump that can be fitted along side a conventional well pump and is claimed to be able to pump to 325 feet. This way while the grid is working the conventional well pump is used and if the grid goes down you can hand pump water to the house. Better yet is the addition of the Simple Pump DC motor which operates the hand pump and can be energized with a relatively small solar panel array. It pumps slowly but it can be used to fill a storage tank.

With a shallow well a narrow bucket can be lowered into the well casing to draw out water. The bucket is actually a pipe with a check valve at the bottom. As it is lowered into the water the check valve permits the bucket to be filled and prevents the water from escaping. These can be purchased or made from inexpensive PVC pipe and fittings. I've thought about combining this idea with a small DC powered capstan to pull the bucket up swiftly. A capstan can be fabricated with an ATV wheel hub turned by a DC motor powered by a battery.

Some properties have artesian wells. A "flowing artesian well" is tapped into an aquifer which is under positive pressure. A well pump is not needed to get access to the water. As expected, a property with an artesian well may come with a high price tag.

Ponds, Rivers, Creeks and Streams

A pond, river, creek or stream can be a good supply of water, especially for livestock or irrigation. If power is available a pump can be placed at the water supply and pumped to wherever it's needed. I would advise filtering any surface water for drinking.

Keep in mind that in most places in America it is unlawful to disrupt or divert a waterway. I would think that if the EPA finds out you are diverting water from a creek (to supply water to livestock for example, with a pump) you will be fined. Who can figure out all the legal bureaucratic red tape involve with such an idea? And the EPA prefers it that way. They simply love to punish people for using natural resources.

Keeping in mind the above, a pond can be created for storage of water that can be used for livestock, irrigation, or firefighting, and in a pinch, drinking water (if properly filtered). But a pond can be expensive to create. It must be excavated, then somehow lined with a a material to prevent the water from seeping into the ground. The material can be a synthetic pond liner, natural clay or a natural material called "Bentonite", which is delivered as a powder but turns into clay when water is added.

I've heard of an old time way to create a pond that saves labor, although it takes time. First the excavation must be done (no way around that!) Then, pigs are to be fenced in the area for a year. Periodically water is sprayed in the pen and the pigs will wallow around in it. After the pigs have spent the entire year trampling the ground, defecating in the pen, and trampling it some more, the bottom of the excavation will become clay-like and impermeable to water. The pigs can be moved and the pit filled with water. I haven't yet tried the idea but many old timers swear by it.

Springs

If a spring is available on the property it can be developed into a water source. Spring water is usually good for drinking if it can be kept from becoming contaminated on the way to the house.

The way to develop a spring is to excavate a small area where you see water seeping from the ground, pour in gravel and dam it up. Install a pipe at the bottom and run this down hill to a small settling tank. Install another pipe from this tank downhill to a storage tank.

A spring may supply less than a gallon per minute, but over the time of a day this can add up to be more than enough water to supply a house. At a half a gallon per minute, that is still over 700 gallons per day. An overflow and drainage will need to be provided because there is no way to shut off the water supply.

If the spring is downhill from the house there is a way to pump the water uphill to a storage tank without using electricity. The device is called a "ram pump" and can be constructed using regularly available steel pipe and fittings and a couple check valves. There is a catch; the water must first flow downhill from the source a minim amount and the piping supplying water to the ram pump must be of steel material. If the ram pump is constantly running it may be able to operate in moderately freezing weather. Alternatively, there are low powered DC solar pumps on the market which can slowly pump the water.

Rainwater Collection

My plans include using the roof as a rain water catchment system. There are a few different reasons for this and the most important reason is that I want to have a source of water without having to depend on the well. The well is reliable but it only works if I have a way to provide 240 volts and 10 amps to the pump. Currently I do this with a generator and I have plans to get enough solar power to energize the well pump, but those ideas depend on either gasoline, oil and spare parts, or complicated fragile electronics. There is the possibility of using some kind of narrow bucket to be lowered with a rope but my well is 500 feet deep!

My area gets between seventeen and eighteen inches of rainfall every year. If I could collect that rain water it could be used to water the livestock, irrigate the garden, used as toilet and shower water, and if filtered, used for cooking and drinking.

When I built the cabin I used steel roofing because it easily sheds contaminants. Asphalt shingles may have some chemicals in them which, in my opinion, may leach into the water. I avoided wood shingles because they seem more likely to be a fire hazard and I didn't want tamarack flavored water.

To find out how much rain water I may collect I had to do some calculations.

First I had to figure out the rain water "catchment area". This aspect of a roof is not the actual "square footage area" of the roof. The area of my roof is 1,152 square feet but the catchment area is slightly smaller because rain falls only on the footprint of the building. Catchment area is the area of the building (not the roof) plus the overhang of the roof.

My building is about 33 feet long and about 25 feet wide, providing an area of 825 feet. The overhang is 2 feet on all four sides, so I could say my catchment area is 29' x 37'. My catchment area is 1,073 square feet.

To calculate how much rain water I can collect from my roof, I multiply the catchment area by one inch of rain and then by the constant 0.623:

$$\text{Catchment Area} \times \text{Rain Water (inches)} \times 0.623 = \text{Gallons of Water Collected}$$

So with every inch of rain I will be able to collect 668 gallons of water! And at 18 inches of rainfall per year I could collect up to 12,000 gallons! This would allow 32 gallons of water every day, assuming it could be collected and stored.

Thirty-two gallons of water per day doesn't seem like much if I include irrigation and livestock water, laundry, daily showers and general usage during conventional times. According to the EPA, the average family of four uses over 400 gallons per day. We don't use nearly that much water at our cabin. Based on how often I fill our water tank, I estimate we use 20-100 gallons per day in the winter depending on how much laundry is washed and how often we shower.

So 32 gallons per day of free rain water would be enough to survive on if I can't depend on the well.

I will need a large storage tank to store the rain water. The tank I am using now holds only 275 gallons. A storage tank needs to be kept in a non-freezing environment or the water in it will eventually freeze. My 275 gallon tank is located inside the cabin in the loft area but I don't have room inside to store a larger tank. When I get the large storage tank I will bury it and use a low powered DC pump to move the water from the large tank to my smaller indoor tank.

The quality of the collected rain water varies with the amount of debris run-off from the roof. This debris can be prevented from entering the tank with a *first flush diverter system*. There are a few manufacturers of this type of system, although I have seen homemade versions. They are passively operated and use no energy and operate on a simple principal. Water in a horizontal pipe must cross a *Tee*. As the first water (and the debris) drops into the Tee, the Tee begins to fill up with water. A buoyant ball in the bottom of the Tee rises to the top as the water level increases. When the ball reaches the top of the Tee and is held there by the water, it plugs the opening to the bottom of the Tee so that the remaining water passes over and continues on its way to the tank. The bottom of the Tee has a small opening to let the water drain out slowly so it is ready for the next rain. A screen can be added at the entrance to the collection tank to catch any remaining debris.

If the water is to be used for drinking it can be filtered. I like the bucket style ceramic filters such as the Big Berkey, but I will add a cartridge type carbon block filter under the kitchen sink. I'm fond of the Pentek line of #10 filter housings which have a 1" inlet, use a 10" x 4-½" filter and can be bought at a reasonable price. I currently use one of those types of filter housings to hold a whole-house sediment filter. A supply of filters could be stockpiled and stored if for some reason they became unavailable.

I've heard of people in New Zealand and Australia who don't filter their rainwater at all and suffer no ill effects drinking it every day. A theory is that they have been doing this their whole lives and have built up immunities to contaminants in the water. It may also be possible that there simply *are no* contaminants in their water. My own feeling is that I wouldn't recommend others drink unfiltered roof water, but I would do it in a heartbeat if things get in such a way that I can't obtain filters.

Since I mentioned rain water collection here, I should mention that last I heard, it was illegal to collect rain water in certain American states.

SHELTER

THERE ARE PEOPLE who might say, 'You have a roof over your head, what else do you really need?'

A shelter is more than a place to get out of the weather. This is where you go after working hard all day. The idea is not to simply *survive*, but to *thrive*. I spent the winter of 2013-2014 in a barely functional shelter, an old camper. It kept me out of the weather and I was able to stay warm (for the most part) but it didn't provide much else. I stayed alive, but it is also important to keep morale up. Especially for those in our family who are not obliged to living in physical hardship. So I learned a few things that should be required in a homestead shelter:

- A hot shower (or bath!) After working all day on improving the homestead, nothing feels better than a hot shower. Somehow it makes everything else acceptable. Try doing hot sweaty work for a few weeks without showering and you'll see what I mean.

- A kitchen. Hot meals are just as important to morale as hot showers. Being able to cook hot meals brings happiness. I was able cook in my camper during the winter of 2013-2014 and it improved morale a great deal.

- A toilet. Especially if females will potentially live at the homestead. Sure you can go outside, but do you really want to do that in the middle of the night when it's ten degrees with a foot of snow on the ground? Even a variation on the "honey bucket" idea will work.

There are a few other things which I don't consider "required" but which will make life much more comfortable:

- Extra insulation and passive solar design. If you can keep cool during summer without using electricity, and keep warm in the winter with a minimal amount of fuel, so much the better. Windows should be on the south with overhangs to keep out the sun in summer but let in sun during the winter. The kitchen should be on the north side of house and bedrooms in cool locations.

- Laundry facilities. I've washed by hand with a wash board and while it does work, it really sucks and I would rather wear filthy clothes. We use an efficient washing machine and hang our clothes to dry them (indoors in the winter).

- Renewable power. Whether it is solar, wind or hydro power, being able to flip a switch and have light is an amazing thing. I currently have a small solar power system, but I am thinking of augmenting it with a wind turbine.

- A root cellar. This is a place to store food without requiring electricity. It takes a lot of electrical power to operate a refrigerator or freezer. Before summer of 2016 I intend to have a root cellar, even if I must hand dig it.

I've gone into great detail about how I built my cabin at minimal cost and using local or re-purposed resources whenever possible. One thing for sure, it is a lot easier to create a nice shelter now rather than wait until we don't have anywhere else to live.

Pioneers built cabins out of the nearby logs and did it all with hand tools. It would probably be a good idea to keep a supply of those tools on hand. Shelter

POWER

E LECTRICITY may not be necessary to survival, but it does make things easier. On my homestead I prefer to have the power now, and prepare to live without it if I need to.

In terms of electrical power, sources are solar, wind turbine, hydro power, and engine-powered devices such as the common gasoline generator. Solar is dependable as long as there is bright sun and the benefit is that there are no moving parts to wear out or break. I believe there is some potential with wind generated power. But I don't think it is reliable except in an area with constant high winds, and due to the moving parts, they require maintenance and occasional repair. Hydro power would probably be the most reliable (although it also requires maintenance and repair), but the location of the running water source must be ideally situated. The location of the creek or stream must be higher in elevation than the location of the generator and there must be a substantial force of water to generate appreciable amounts of power.

Generators

Our property is off grid. The nearest electrical connection is miles away. That meant we had to make some big adjustments to our lifestyles. We still use electricity, but not as much as most people in the US. We have a small solar power system but we still use generators a lot. We could get away with less use, but for now we sometimes run a generator all day long. In the aim of self reliance, in the future I hope to reduce my dependence on generators almost completely. But for now we are stuck with them.

I never owned a generator before moving to the homestead. Being of the preparedness mind set, I had wanted one, but could not justify the cost. I never dreamed I would have three generators at one time.

I bought the first generator from Harbor Freight because it was on sale for $90. I think it was an 800 watt unit. I don't remember for sure because something broke in the recoil mechanism before I could get it started. I got my money back.

I got the second generator from Amazon.com for around $400. A 3500 watt Duromax (4400 max watts) with electric start which we ran hard for a year. I mean like 10 hours per day. I have to say that I never even changed the oil on that genny. I had to add oil every week so it seemed like it wasn't worth it to change the oil because it changed itself. Where all that oil went I don't know. But she had a 240 volt outlet and could run the well pump, so all things considering Ol' Blue did a pretty good job.

But after that first year, Ol' Blue broke and wouldn't start. I tinkered with it but small engines were not my area of expertise so I did some online shopping and drove all the way to Lowes in Spokane to get a Generac GP3300 for $429. But when I got there, I noticed they had a Troy-Bilt 5500 on clearance, new, in the unopened box, for $314. This was a generator that normally costs $768. I snatched it up, and considering my experience with Ol' Blue, I got the Lowes Extended Protection Plan for another $50.

Big Red was awesome, started on the first pull (no electric start) and was able to run my air compressor nail gun and big Rigid miter saw. I used Big Red plenty while building the cabin. By then we had some solar panels and didn't abuse Big Red as much as we did Ol' Blue, who was now sitting in the weeds at the well, abandoned. I loved Big Red so much I even occasionally changed the oil if I thought about it. I put a bigger set of wheels on Big Red so I could move him around easier.

After we had Big Red for almost a year he stopped producing voltage. Not cause for a real panic because we had the Extended Protection Plan. But by now my wife and kids were living with me, and my 16 year old daughter was going to school every weekday. With Big Red being repaired, we had no way to get water from the well, so my poor daughter wouldn't be able to take a shower for school!

My wife took Big Red back to Lowes and they said it would take at least two weeks to get him repaired. My wife explained our situation. She is persuasive. The manager at Lowes agreed to give my wife a great deal on the Generac GP3300 (a $429 generator) for $300 so we could get by while Big Red was being repaired! So my wife brought home Orange Crush.

Naturally, my wife had gotten the Extended Protection Plan for the new generator. Orange Crush is a cute li'l thing and the first thing we figured out after I put bigger wheels on her is that she won't run the well pump! The Generac GP3300 has the 20-amp 240 volt receptacle that won't fit the 30-amp plug on the well.

I spent the next morning shopping the local hardware stores (2 within 60 miles) for an adapter or plug. No luck. So I spent the next few hours working on Ol' Blue again. I know that a no-start situation is always a problem of either no spark or no gas. I narrowed it down to the ignition. Replaced the spark plug boot and wire with a spare from the tractor, reset the gap on the coil, and Ol' Blue fired right up! I was astounded at my own ability! Well, youtube helped a lot.

So I moved Ol' Blue back to the well and we were able to get water. This meant Orange Crush could be left at the camper and we wouldn't have to haul a generator to the well pump every day to fill up the camper water tank.

But I had no way to run my nail gun or miter saw, so I hand sawed and hand nailed for weeks while we waited for Big Red to get fixed. Then 3 weeks went by and my wife got on the phone with Lowes, got a manager, and found out Big Red hadn't yet been shipped out to get fixed!

My wife explained our situation. As I said, she is persuasive. The manager agreed to give us a new comparable generator. But the only comparable generator they had was the Generac 5500 watt. My wife said she didn't want a Generic.

"None of that Chinese crap", she said, although I tried to tell her from the background that they are all made in China. She told the manager that we had bought a Troy-Bilt, and if she couldn't have Big Red back she "wanted a new Troy-Bilt with the Briggs and Stratton engine!"

I was in the background saying, "I don't care if it's a Generac!", but when she is being "persuasive" nothing can stop her. The Lowes manager told my wife that he understands, and he can give us a Troy-Bilt 7000 watt as a replacement for Big Red.

The next day my wife went to Lowes and came home with this monster generator which has a price tag of $899, only she didn't pay a nickel for it. She even got my old wheels back, which I installed on the new genny as soon as she brought it home.

The new generator, who I call Red Bull, is a real beast. Weighs 171 pounds empty and really drinks the gas compared to Orange Crush. It has this neat extension cable with an information panel.

While we were still living in the camper we left Red Bull at the cabin so I could use him for power tools and I left Orange Crush at the camper. I left Ol' Blue at the well.

Long story short, we had three working generators. Red Bull is a $899 generator, but we got him as a replacement for a $768 generator for which we paid $314 on clearance. And Orange Crush is a $429 generator we got for $300. And we still have Ol' Blue which has again refused to start and I think its a simple problem of a dead battery. But she was acting up for awhile before that. At some point I'm going to have to look at her again.

I would like to someday get one of those 1800 RPM Lister generators that run on diesel and maybe someday I will. But in the mean time I will buy my small generators from Lowes and I will always get the Extended Protection Plan.

Introduction to Solar Power

The camper had standard RV batteries and I bought a 600 Watt pure sine wave inverter so we could run 120 volt items like the TV and computers. On rainy days the TV was on for a good part of the day. The inverter worked fine, but it drained the batteries too quickly. Eventually we purchased two L16 380 Amp hour 6 volt off-grid batteries to replace the old RV batteries. I connected them in series to output 12 Volts DC.

Eventually we decided to add some solar panels. This would allow us to take some of the load off the generator so we wouldn't have to run it as often saving wear and tear, and fuel. The plan was to start small and add on as we can. That is not the preferred way to go about building a solar power system, but we never seemed to have enough money to spend on a big system; especially when we had to put most of our money towards materials and tools to make the property livable and to build a house.

I spent a lot of time researching how to design a solar power system. Once upon a time I was an electrician in the military, so I was familiar with electrical concepts. But I still had a lot of learning to do. I will not call myself an expert on solar power, but I did learn a lot from places like the Northern Arizona Wind & Sun[1] forum on the internet. The good folks there were very helpful.

There are four basic components to a solar power system, listed below in order of decreasing expense:

1. Battery bank
2. Solar Panels
3. DC-AC Inverter
4. Charge Controller

---

1 *Forum - Solar Electric Power. Northern Arizona Wind & Sun, n.d. Web. 3 Jan. 2015.* <http://forum.solar-electric.com/forum.php>.

But before we can decide what equipment we need, we must first determine the size of the system. There are four simple steps to follow to design a solar power system:

1. Determine the size of the electrical loads per day, in Watt-Hours

2. Determine the size of the battery bank required to supply the electrical load

3. Calculate the charging current and voltage required for the battery bank

4. Calculate the size of the solar panel array to provide the charging current

The formulas I use are below.

First, a note about connecting batteries:

To connect two batteries together in a *series string* means the positive terminal on one battery is connected to the negative terminal on the other battery, and the load is connected to the remaining negative and positive terminals.

To connect two batteries together in a *parallel string* means the two positive terminals are connected together, and the two negative terminals are connected together. The load is connected to the positive terminal on one battery and the negative terminal on the other battery.

The series-parallel connections can be made on any number of batteries and can be combined, but typically there are no more than six batteries in a parallel string.

Basic Formulas & Notes:

Watt = Amps x Volts

Watt-Hours = Watts x Hours

Battery Bank System Voltage = 12 Volts, 24 Volts or 48 Volts

Max Depth of Discharge = .25 (converted from 25%; this number can be changed by the user)

Formulas To Determine Required Battery Bank Specs:

Daily Watt-Hour Use = Total Watt-Hours used each day

Required Battery Bank Capacity in Watt-Hours = Daily Watt-Hour Use ÷ Max Depth of Discharge

Required Battery Bank Capacity in Amp-Hours = Required Battery Bank Capacity in Watt-Hours ÷ Battery Bank System Voltage

Formulas To Determine Actual Battery Bank Specs:

Battery Bank Capacity in Amp-Hours = Number of Batteries Connected in Parallel x Individual Battery Amp-Hour Rating

Actual Battery Bank Capacity in Watt-Hours = Battery Bank Capacity in Amp-Hours x Battery Voltage

Battery Charge Voltage *Per Cell* = Manufacturer's Specifications

Quantity of (Battery Bank) Cells = Battery Bank System Voltage ÷ 2 (usually)

Battery Bank Charge Voltage = Quantity of Cells x Charge Voltage Per Cell

Battery Bank Charge Current = Battery Bank Capacity in Amp-Hours x 10%

Formulas To Determine Solar Panel Array Size:

Solar Array Derating Factor = .77 (systems are 77% efficient)

Solar Panel Array size, in Watts = Battery Bank Charge Voltage x Battery Bank Charge Current ÷ **Solar Array Derating Factor**

Example:

I'm going to design an example solar power system. Before I can use the formulas I have to gather some information. I've measured my daily electrical use and came up with 1,140 Watt-Hours. I decided on a battery system voltage and looked up the specs for some batteries. Here is what I know about my requirements and the batteries. Keep in mind that I haven't *yet* used any formulas.

Daily Watt-Hour Use = **1,140**

Max Depth of Discharge = 25%

Battery Bank System Voltage (estimated) = 12

Battery type (each, manufacturer's specs) = 6 Volt

Quantity of Battery Cells (each, manufacturer's specs) = 3

Battery Amp-Hour rating (each, manufacturer's specs) = 380

Battery Charge Voltage Per Cell (manufacturer's specs) = 2.45

Now I begin to use the formulas. First I find my *Required Battery Bank Capacity in Watt-Hours.*

Required Battery Bank Capacity in Watt-Hours = Daily Watt-Hour Use ÷ Max Depth of Discharge

1,140 ÷ .25 (25%) = **4,560 Watt-Hours**

Then I calculate the *Required Battery Bank Capacity in Amp-Hours:*

Required Battery Bank Capacity in Amp-Hours = Required Battery Bank Capacity in Watt-Hours ÷ Battery Bank System Voltage

4,560 ÷ 12 = 380 Amp-Hours

Then I find my *Battery Bank Charge Voltage.*

Quantity of Battery Bank Cells = Battery Bank System Voltage ÷ 2

12 ÷ 2 = **6 Cells** (I verified this anyway with the manufacturer's specs)

Battery Bank Charge Voltage = Quantity of Cells x Charge Voltage Per Cell

6 x 2.45 = **14.7 Volts**

Next I'll calculate the Battery Bank Charge Current.

Battery Bank Charge Current = Battery Bank Capacity in Amp-Hours x 10%

380 x 0.10 = 38 Amps

Finally, I will calculate the Solar Panel Array Size.

Solar Panel Array Size, in Watts = Battery Bank Charge Voltage x Battery Bank Charge Current ÷ Solar Array Derating Factor

1.7 x 38 ÷ .77 = 725 Watts

Conclusion:

So it looks like I will need a 380 Amp-Hour battery bank and at least 725 watts in solar panels to charge them with. This should support my 1,140 Watt-Hours that I use every day, with a max battery discharge rate of 25%.

Final Thoughts

"The unexamined life is not worth living"
~ Socrates

ANY ADVICE I have given is based on my own observations, experiences and research. I don't claim to be an expert on any subject I have touched upon in this book. There are a thousand ways to build a house and there will be people who will disagree with the way I constructed my cabin. I am comfortable in my feeling that it is safe and will be around for a long time but I won't recommend to anyone that they build their house exactly like I did.

Building a homestead is a personal experience and this book outlines my journey of discovery. I learned about homesteading, but more importantly I learned about myself. It is my hope that someone may read my story and see that it *is* possible; we can do anything if we put our minds to it.

My homestead is not finished and sometimes I feel as if my work has only just begun. There is still a lot to do. The work seems like it will never end but I don't mind.

I am at the place where I want to be and the work that comes is *my* work. And I am here to do it.

Bibliography

Recommended Reading

Deppe, Carol. *The Resilient Gardener: Food Production and Self-reliance in Uncertain times*. White River Junction, VT: Chelsea Green Pub., 2010. Print. <http://www.amazon.com/dp/160358031X>

Guthrie, A. B. *The Big Sky: A Novel*. Boston: Houghton Mifflin, 2002. Print. <http://www.amazon.com/dp/0618154639>

Hemenway, Toby. *Gaia's Garden: A Guide to Home-scale Permaculture*. White River Junction, VT: Chelsea Green Pub., 2009. Print. <http://www.amazon.com/dp/1603580298>.

Jacke, Dave, and Eric Toensmeier. *Edible Forest Gardens, Vol II*. White River Junction, VT: Chelsea Green Pub., 2005. Print. <http://www.amazon.com/dp/1931498806>.

Jenkins, Joseph C. *The Humanure Handbook: A Guide to Composting Human Manure*. Grove City, PA: Joseph Jenkins, 2005. Print. <http://www.amazon.com/dp/0964425831>

Logsdon, Gene. *The Gardener's Guide to Better Soil*. Emmaus, PA: Rodale, 1975. Print. <http://www.amazon.com/dp/087857106X>

Ludwig, Art. *The New Create an Oasis with Greywater. ; Choosing, Building, and Using Greywater Systems, Includes Branched Drains*. N.p.: Oasis Design, 2006. Print. <http://www.amazon.com/dp/0964343398>

Shein, Christopher, and Julie Thompson. *The Vegetable Gardener's Guide to Permaculture: Creating an Edible Ecosystem*. Portland, Or.: Timber, 2013. Print. <http://www.amazon.com/dp/1604692707>.

Solomon, Steve. *Gardening When It Counts Growing Food in Hard times*. England: New Society (PA), 2006. Print. <http://www.amazon.com/dp/086571553X>

Ussery, Harvey. *The Small-scale Poultry Flock: An All-natural Approach to Raising Chickens and Other Fowl for Home and Market Growers*. White River Junction, VT: Chelsea Green, 2011. Print. <http://www.amazon.com/dp/1603582908>.

Vendors & Reports

Axmen. *Axmen*. <http://www.axmen.com>. 7655 US Highway 10 W, Missoula, MT 59808, 406-728-7020

Cooks Saw Mfg., LLC. *Bandsaw Blades*. <https://www.cookssaw.com/index.php/bandsaw-blades>. 160 Ken Lane, Newton, AL 36352, 1-800-473-4804.

"SQ Series Pumps." *SQ | Grundfos*. N.p., n.d. Web. 3 Jan. 2015. <http://www.grundfos.com/products/find-product/sq.html>.

"Grundfos SQFlex." *Grundfos*. N.p., n.d. Web. 3 Jan. 2015. <http://us.grundfos.com/products/find-product/sqflex.html>.

"NASS - Montana Publications and Press Releases." *NASS - Montana Publications and Press Releases*. U.S. Department of Agriculture, n.d. Web. 3 Jan. 2015. <http://www.nass.usda.gov/Statistics_by_State/Montana/Publications>.

Forum - Solar Electric Power. Northern Arizona Wind & Sun, n.d. Web. 3 Jan. 2015. <http://forum.solar-electric.com/forum.php>.

Acknowledgments

I wouldn't be where I am today without the help of many other people.

Starting with my father, Wayne who taught me the value of hard work, and my mother, Sara, who gave me a love of reading.

Tina, Brandon, Troy, and Haleigh, mean everything to me.

The generosity of my wife's parents, Scotty and Susan, was overwhelming.

My friends Steve and Judy have helped me more times than I can count.

Thanks to all.

About the Author

Gordon Blaine is a proud descendant of the Amish. He lives off the grid in the mountains of Montana in a cabin he built with his wife and children. As a former member of the United States military and later as a military contractor, he traveled the United States and the world. But his greatest influences are his father, who instilled in him an appreciation of generosity and integrity, and his mother, who gave him his sense of humor and a love of literature.

CPSIA information can be obtained
at www.ICGtesting.com
Printed in the USA
LVOW13s1109050517
533384LV00020B/741/P

9 781506 155951